AUTHOR

Since 2009, Chris Flaherty has written for the UK Armourer Magazine; Classic Arms & Militaria; and, Soldiers of the Queen Journal. He has advised major international museums on uniforms. For Partizan Press in 2014, he wrote and illustrated two books: 'Turkish Uniforms of the Crimean War: A Handbook of Uniforms'; and, 'The Ottoman Army in the First World War: A Handbook of Uniforms'. He co-authored and illustrated with Bruno Mugnai for Soldiershop Publishing: 2014 'Der Lange Turkenkrieg (1593-1606), Volume. 1: The Long Turkish – War Habsburg Arrests the Ottoman Advance; and, in 2015 'Der Lange Turkenkrieg (1593- 1606), Volume. 2: The Long Turkish War'. In 2015, he was a contributor (illustrator) to the Turkish Gallipoli Centenary Exhibition: 'From Depths to the Trenches: Gallipoli 1915', at the Isbank Museum in Istanbul. He was one of the contributors to, 'Philip Jowett, 2015 Armies of the Greek-Turkish War 1919–22', Men-at-Arms 50, Osprey Publishing. He authored a chapter on the, 'Ottoman Army in the Great Northern War' appearing in Stephen, L. Kling, Jr. (Editor) 2016 GNW Compendium: A Collection of Articles on the Great Northern War, 1700-1721 (Volume: 2), The Historical Game Company. Chris Flaherty has authored and illustrated for Partizan Press' Universal Wargames Rules Supplements: 'Napoleonic Small Siege, River Ship, Gunboat and Pontooning' (2016); 'Napoleonic Foraging, Insurrection, Marauders, Bakeries, Convoy and Encampment Wargaming' (2016); 'Napoleonic Balloon Warfare' (2017); 'Napoleonic Ottoman Army Wargaming Supplement' (2018); 'A Wargamer's Guide to WW1 Ottoman Army Uniforms' (2018); 'Napoleon's July 1798 Pyramid Campaign & the Egyptian Army' (2019); 'The Napoleonic Ottoman Army: Uniforms, Tactics and Organization' (2019). Over 2021 and 2022 he wrote and illustrated several titles for Soldiershop Publishing, including: 'The Sardinian Expeditionary Corps'.

PUBLISHER'S NOTES

None of unpublished images or text of our book may be reproduced in any format without the expressed written permission of Soldiershop.com when not indicate as marked with license creative commons 3.0 or 4.0. Soldiershop Publishing has made every reasonable effort to locate, contact and acknowledge rights holders and to correctly apply terms and conditions to Content. In the event that any Content infringes your rights or the rights of any third parties, or Content is not properly identified or acknowledged we would like to hear from you so we may make any necessary alterations. In this event contact: info@soldiershop.com. Our trademark: Soldiershop Publishing ©, The names of our series & brand: Museum book, Bookmoon, Soldiers&Weapons, Battlefield, War in colour, Historical Biographies, Darwin's view, Fabula, Altrastoria, Italia Storica Ebook, Witness To History, Soldiers, Weapons & Uniforms, Storia etc. are herein © by Soldiershop.com.

LICENSES COMMONS

This book may utilize part of material marked with license creative commons 3.0 or 4.0 (CC BY 4.0), (CC BY-ND 4.0), (CC BY-SA 4.0) or (CC0 1.0). Or derived from publication 70 years old or more and recolored from us. We give appropriate attribution credit and indicate if change were made in the acknowledgements field.
All our books utilize only fonts licensed under the SIL Open Font License or other free use license.

ISBN: 9791255890393 1st edition October 2023
S&W-050 - LATE 18th CENTURY TURKISH CAVALRY
Written and illustrated by Chris Flaherty
Editor: Luca Cristini Editore, for the brand: Soldiershop. Cover & Art Design: Luca S. Cristini.

CHRIS FLAHERTY

LATE 18ᵀᴴ CENTURY TURKISH CAVALRY

UNIFORMS, TACTICS AND ORGANIZATION

SOLDIERS&WEAPONS 050

CONTENTS

INTRODUCTION..5

Chapter 1: Sultan's Household Guard..8

Chapter 2: Zirkhli..13

Chapter 3: Provincial Sipahi Light Cavalry and Lancers...................19

Chapter 4: Deli..24

Chapter 5: Topracly and Mounted Infantry..28

Chapter 6: Mameluke..31

Chapter 7: Bedouin...48

Chapter 8: Tatar..53

Chapter 9: Sipahi Sornazen...58

Chapter 10: Traditional Cavalry Role in Battle..................................59

Chapter 11: Sultan's Household Guard Banners, Officers' Command Flags and Lance Pennants..67

Chapter 12: Weapons, Equipment and Horse Furniture.....................72

Bibliography..78

INTRODUCTION

During the June 1806 New Order Army Regulars' Edirne campaign, under Kadi Abdurrahman Pasha[1], the Regulars was primarily an Infantry force of some 22,685 Soldiers[2,3], that rose to 24,000 with Cavalry sent by Anatolian nobles: Karaosmanoglu and Capanoglu [Cabbaroglus] family dynasties. The Family Regiments Cavalry were likely to have been Trained Mounted Infantry from the Uskudar Barracks (the second Regimental-formation of the Nizam-i Cedid [Nizam-i Cedit; Nizam-i Jedid]: New Order Army), that may have amounted to around 500 Soldiers each. The 1806 New Order Army composition suggests a radical departure from traditional Turkish warfare practices, that placed a heavy reliance on mainly Cavalry-based Armies. In the late 18th Century, the main offensive combat component of the Kapikulu Ocaklari: Standing Army was its Sipahi: Cavalry. Cavalry numbers used by Turkish Armies were large. For instance, at the Battle of Forhani in 1789, the Austrian and Russian advancing Corps faced large-scale Sipahi attacks, of 15,000 from their left, and then 20,000 from their right flanks, which were well ahead of 5,000 at the most Infantry, left to defend the major entrenched camp[4]. Sipahi accompanying the Army into Egypt appear to have been a large force of 25,000 Soldiers[5]. While at the Battle of Heliopolis in 1800, a Sipahi charge was known to have consisted of 20,000 Soldiers[6]. By the time of the British and Allied investment of Cairo and Giza, the Turkish Army under the Grand Vizier, was similarly favored toward its Cavalry component, with about 12,000 Cavalry Soldiers, and only 7,000 Infantry[7].

STANDING ARMY CAVALRY ORGANIZATION

The basis of Turkish military organization underpinning the existence of the Standing Army was the enrolment system, where Soldiers were enrolled into the legers of various orders, like the Janissary, or the Sipahi, and were guaranteed yearly, or quarterly wages by the State, or access to income-earning estates: Timar fiefs. As enrollment was life-long, enrollees were further distinguished into categories: militarily active, too old to fight, or pensioners. The main Cavalry types seen during the late 18th Century were: Sultan's Household Guard Regiments; Zirkhli: Cuirassier - Armoured Sipahi, who wore metal helmets, and chainmail shirts; Sipahi Light Cavalry or Lancers; Deli; Mameluke, who were largely organized into Zirkhli, Light Cavalry, or Cameleers; Bedouin Light Cavalry; and, Tatar Light Cavalry, that were divided into Vanguard Troops of the Turkish Army (Tatar of Circassia), and Ottoman-Dobruca Tatar Provisional Military Units. New Order Army military reforms of Sultan Selim III (1789 till 1807), had by start of the Napoleonic Wars added to the Standing Army the following Mounted Infantry and Cavalry:

Karaosmanoglu Family Cavalry:	Provincial Regiments (500 each), of Uskudar Barracks Trained Mounted Infantry.
Capanoglu Family Cavalry:	
Paid Mounted Regulars Light Cavalry or Lancers:	10,000 Soldiers organized into ten Provincial Sipahi Alay: Regiments (1,000 each).

Following formation of the 1826 Mansure Army, under Sultan Mahmud II, the traditional Sipahi Alay: Regiments remained till 1828 when these were retired, and new Turkish Army Cavalry Regulars were raised.

---

1 Creasy, 1878.
2 Shaw, 1965.
3 Aksan, 2007.
4 Anthing, 1813.
5 Morier, 1801.
6 Alison, 1842.
7 Wittman, 1803.

CAVALRY COMMAND

Notwithstanding the large number of Sipahi used, Cavalry organization was simple. Only a few Officers led any Cavalry formation, and was noted, "so 10-11,000 Soldiers were led by fifteen Officers[8]". The following Officers were known:

Agha [Aga]:	Commander of Cavalry
Alay Bey (or Bimbashi: Leader of a Thousand):	Commander of a Provincial Alay: Regiment
Subasis:	Captain of a Left or Right Wing
Boluk Leader:	Sub-Files

On campaign, the Alay: a 1,000 Soldier strong Regiment was used as the basis for the Provincial Sipahi organization[9]. Each Provincial Sipahi Alay was, "commanded by an Alay Bey."[10] However, the rank of Bimbashi: Leader of a Thousand, related to Infantry command of Orta: Battalions, that became a key New Order Army Infantry rank of Battalion Major, also appears to have extended to command within the Cavalry earlier in the 18th Century. A 1773 account of the Russian-Turkish War records an attack on Russian troops by, "a body of … [Sipahi] … who had upwards of four hundred men, left … a few prisoners, among whom was their … [Bimbashi] … an aged venerable man."[11] Provincial Sipahi Alay were further divided, under the command of three or four Subasis: Captains[12]. These Officers were likely the Sub-Leaders of traditional Attack Divisions of an Alay, that would divide into, namely – Right, Centre, and Left Divisions. Junior Cavalry Officers were Boluk Leaders. The Boluk: File or Section, was the Sub-Tactical Unit. It could be as low as eight, or ten Soldiers, but could be as high as 25 to 30[13].

Under military reforms of Sultan Selim III, each New Order Army Infantry Buluk: Company had a Sornazen: Trumpeter, and Tablzen: Drummer[14]. It is possible that Sultan Selim III's force of 10,000 Paid Mounted Regulars were organized into ten Provincial Sipahi Alay, and were similarly organized to the New Order Army. Depicted in the 1810 Sultan Mahmud II Grand Review[15], is Light Cavalry all wearing the same uniforms, led by an Officer, Alemdar: Flag Bearer Officer (under the New Order Army Regulars organization), and a Sornazen: Trumpeter (also established under the New Order Army).

AGA OF THE CAVALRY

An 1805 illustration of the, "Aga General der Reuterey": General of the Cavalry[16], show a low collared long gold pattern gown with red waist sash worn under a long red fur-lined coat with short wide sleeves (some versions show high ranking Turkish Officers with additional long double sleeves). A tall brown and purple candy-striped wide-topped cylindrical peakless fez-styled hat with a tall white horsehair plume secured by a gilt rosette, and red Turkish riding boots complete the dress. The General is depicted carrying a Topuz [Gurz]: mace – a symbol of authority. Commonly part of Sipahi equipment[17]. Topuz were used as an insignia of inauguration, and symbol of the Sultan's military authority[18].

8	Hammer-Purgstall, 1837.
9	Hammer-Purgstall, 1837.
10	Johnson, 1988.
11	Unknown, 1799.
12	Hammer-Purgstall, 1837.
13	Hammer-Purgstall, 1837.
14	Shaw, 1965.
15	Unknown, 1810.
16	Unknown, 1805.
17	Uyar, 2009.
18	Ocak, 2016.

It is known, "quality and the decoration of the mace reflected the rank of the holder: the heavier and more decorated the mace, the more honorable the person who had it."[19] The Aga horse furniture was equally sumptuous, consisting of a blue with extensive silver floral embroidery padded saddle incorporating a large square saddle cloth-cover edged with a blue long-thick knotted tassel fringe. A wide blue harness chest strap, with gold metal badges and large gold metal side pendants, with three blue long-thick knotted tassels. The red leather harness and reins had gold metal fittings, and decorated with gold metal pendants with long-thick forelock knotted tassels. The horse's tail was tied with a blue bow.

FIGURE 1: Aga of the Cavalry, and Tug: three horse-tails standard used to show rank.

---
19   Ocak, 2016.

CHAPTER 1: SULTAN'S HOUSEHOLD GUARD

The main Sultan's Household Guard Cavalry organization, known as the Suvarileri [Buluk Halki]: Regiment Men[20], was organized into six Divisions, said to have constituted some 28,000 Soldiers. However, it is not known how many of these enrollees were militarily active. The six Divisions were identified as:

Kapikulu Sipahi [Spahi]	Cavalry of the Porte (Sultan): An elite Regiment granted Timar fiefs near Constantinople, alongside their salaries.
Silahtar [Silahdar]	An elite Regiment known as Weapon Masters or Weapons Bearers. Traditionally were the Sultan's Personal Guard. Largely composed of former Janissary Infantry, they were granted Timar fiefs near Constantinople, alongside their salaries.
Right-Ulufecis	Salaried Ones: Zirkhli: Cuirassier - Armoured Sipahi, who wore full body suits of Indian-Persian armour.
Left-Ulufecis	
Right-Garips	Poor Ones: Salaried Regiments of lightly equipped troops.
Left-Garips	

Janissary could become a Silahtar [Silahdar] if promoted for bravery, via the Ztrhli Nefer: Armoured Janissary Infantry, who operated in small - 30 to 100 strong bands of hand-picked Soldiers. Wearing the best and heaviest armour, including the round iron-steel plate shield, Ztrhli Nefer during sieges, or on the open battlefield would engage in near-suicidal missions. It is said that other members of the Division, with Cavalry backgrounds, would despise him and former comrade Janissary considered him a traitor, but because the position and wealth of a Silahtar was so attractive, a Janissary would still enlist for dangerous missions with the hope of joining the Cavalry. Baltadji [Baltadjis; Baltaci]: Axe-man, woodcutter, pioneer, or halberdier were also known to have been able to enroll in the Kapikulu Sipahi and Silahtar Regiments.

Silahtar, many of whom were former Janissary, may have displayed a Janissary plume or spoon holder on their helmets, if they were wearing full traditional armour, dressed as Zirkhli: Cuirassier - Armoured Sipahi. By the 18th Century, Guard Cavalry where likely dressed like the rest of the Zirkhli, or Sipahi except that their clothing, weapons and horse furniture was made of richer materials.

SULTAN SELIM III MOUNTED GUARDS REGIMENTS

The 1796 General Aubert du Bayet Military Mission trained from the Mounted Lifeguards two Cavalry Squadrons[21]. Training produced the Light Horse a l'Europeenne. Under Sultan Selim III, a new unit, the Elite Sipahi [Spahi] Oglans: Children of the Kapikulu Sipahi [Spahi] were also raised as his Personal Bodyguard Regiment[22]. There was also an Albanian Guard Cavalry and three Mameluke Regiments:

	POSSIBLE UNIT STRENGTH:
Elite Sipahi [Spahi] Oglans: Children of the Kapikulu Sipahi [Spahi]: Sultan Selim III's Personal Bodyguard Regiment:	Alay: Cavalry Regiment (1,000 Soldiers)
Mounted Lifeguards: Light Horse a l'Europeenne:	Two French Army-styled Squadrons
Albanian Guard Cavalry:	Alay: Cavalry Regiment (1,000)

20	Johnson, 1988.
21	Roubicek, 1978.
22	Johnson, 1988.

Mameluke of Constantinople Regiment:	Alay: Cavalry Regiment (1,000)
Mameluke of Grand Seignior [Sultan]'s Regiment:	Alay: Cavalry Regiment (1,000)
Mameluke of the Grand Vizier's Regiment:	Alay: Cavalry Regiment (1,000)

A later 1829 Traveler's account, described the uniforms of a Corps, called: "Light Horse a l'Europeenne", which likely reflected the same or similar uniform worn since the time of Sultan Selim III, being the earlier Mounted Lifeguards, in 1796:

> "Their uniform was simple and good: they wore a close blue jacket, with a little embroidery in yellow worsted, blue Cossack … [trousers] … and black leather boots with spurs screwed to the heels. Their cap was the same red skull-cap with a blue tassel, as worn by the Infantry"[23].

ALBANIAN GUARD CAVALRY

An illustration depicting a, "Turkish Officer of the Sipahi"[24], is similar to another, from 1810[25], and 1818, identified as a, "Soldier of Albania", or "Officer of Spahis"[26]. Metal band leggings points to the Napoleonic Era, and possibly Arnaut: Albanian as the origin. An account from an English Diplomat who accompanied the Turkish Army into Egypt, in 1800, noted in relation to some Albanian Infantry wearing, "a species of armour … [covering] … their legs"[27]. It is suspected, these are Napoleonic Era, and are a special mounted Arnaut: Albanian Regiment in the Sultan's Household Cavalry, wearing what appears to be a Turkish version of a Grenadier's cap made from red cloth, with gold tape decorated headband, and the front displaying a long gold metal badge with tall red feathers coming from the top. A white collarless buttoned (with large round silver metal buttons) long coat, with short sleeves with broad red tape ends, is worn over a white collarless shirt with tight-fitting long sleeves. A red and white striped skirt, or apron covers the legs down to the knees. Red Turkish slipper-shoes with white socks complete the dress. Despite their somewhat archaic appearance, the large square shields slung over the back may be a further example of Arnaut: Albanian troops using items of dress that gives them a distinctly classical Greek (or Roman) appearance. The Albanian Guard Cavalry Soldier's saddle and horse furniture is illustrated in, "Turkish Cavalry" that dates between 1809 till 1813[28], and in an earlier illustration of, "Turkische Cavallerie" hand dated 1795[29], and this shows a heavily white fringed light-blue square saddle cloth with double white tape edges. A Type of pistol holster can be seen, and this is covered with pink cloth edged with wide gold tape. A wide red harness chest strap, with white edges, and decorated with white crescents, and chevrons displays a gold badge and red horse tail pendant. A similar design neck halter with gold knotted tassels, and red horse tail pendant, formed part of the red leather harness and reins, which are decorated with gold fixtures.

23	MacFarlane, 1829.
24	Kobell, 1813.
25	Unknown, 1810.
26	McLean, 1818.
27	Morier, 1801.
28	Kobell, 1813.
29	Unknown, 1795.

FIGURE 2: Paid Mounted Regulars Light Cavalry Officer (1810).

FIGURE 3: Paid Mounted Regulars Light Cavalry Soldier (1810).

FIGURE 4: Sultan's Albanian Guard Cavalry Soldier, with details for armoured leg coverings, and alternative pennant without crescent badge (1800 till 1810).

CHAPTER 2: ZIRKHLI

Zirkhli: Cuirassier, the Armoured Sipahi of the 18th Century and Napoleonic Era, had undergone a considerable change since the 16th and 17th Centuries. It appears likely that only a few Alay: Regiments were equipped as Zirkhli. It may have been that most of the Zirkhli were Mameluke. It is also the case Zirkhli known to exist may have been retained by the Sultan's Household Guard's two Regiments Right, and Left -Ulufecis: Salaried Ones, who were equipped as Zirkhli-Armoured Sipahi, wearing full body suits of Indian-Persian armour. The historical question is what was the number of the Zirkhli? In the case of the Khedive's Egyptian Army, it maintained a three-Squadron Regiment of Zirkhli Bodyguard, from the 1830s[30]. They were traditionally known in Egypt as the Zirkhagi: Iron Men.

BODY ARMOUR

An illustration of a Zirkhli[31], while likely to date from Sultan Mustafa II (1695 to 1703), or Sultan Ahmed III (1703 to 1730), could still represent a Heavy Cavalry Soldier well past 1750. The Soldier wears the familiar full-body suit of Indian-Persian chainmail and plate armour. Forearm plate covers, and upper legs and knees covered with armoured plate, with Turkish long yellow leg covering riding boots completing the dress. It should be noted, that a near identical type of Soldier, called Tribal Cataphract Heavy Cavalry was still retained in the Qajar-Persian Army, till late in the 19th Century.

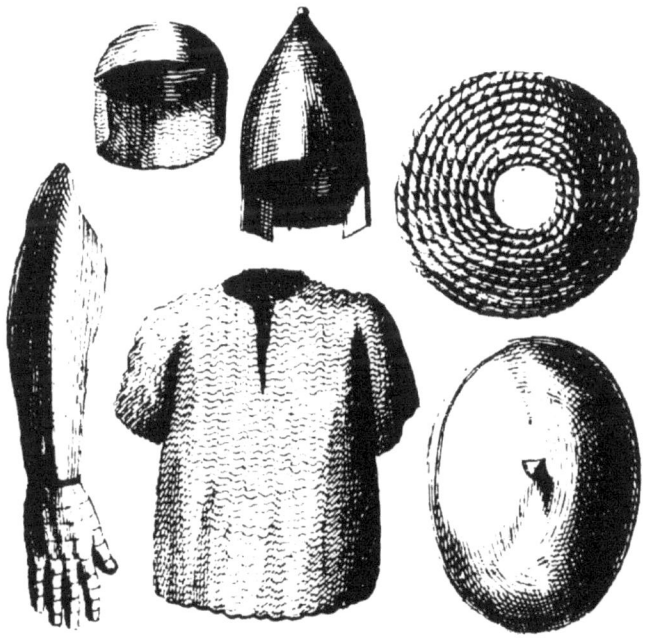

▲ A 1732 illustration of Turkish Heavy Cavalry Armour[32]. This consisted of open face helmets of various designs, right-arm shield made from iron-steel plate, with a boss-spike, or wickerwork shield made from spirally plaited cane, incorporating an iron boss, short-sleeved chainmail shirt, and left-forearm plate cover, and armoured gauntlet.

---

30   Dunn, 2013.
31   Sevket, 1907.
32   Marsigli, 1732.

Chainmail Shirts

It is known that 18th Century Turkish still used chainmail armour; after the Battle of Heliopolis in Egypt, in 1800, when French raided the main Turkish camp, it was said: "Among other valuables found in the camp, were a great number of coats of mail, and iron helmets."[33] The 18th Century European fashion equipping Heavy Cavalry with steel cuirass, even the demi-version (front plate only), was never seen in Turkish Armies. Zirkhli wore a collarless chainmail top shirt with short sleeves, and short skirt ending below the waist, that had a short slit-opening at the front of the collar[34,35], was all that remained of full-suits of Turkish, and Indian-Persian armour worn in the previous Centuries. This lacked metal plate abdomen reinforcement, commonly seen on 16th, or 17th Centuries Indian-Persian chainmail long-sleeved shirts.

▲ An 1732 illustration of a chainmail shirt[36,37]

It is also possible that collarless, and cloth covered sleeveless chainmail over-vest developed. An 1803 illustration of a Mameluke Zirkhli[38], one from 1812[39], and a version seen in, "Turkish Cavalry" that dates between 1809 till 1813[40], show wearing a green cloth collarless tight-fitting sleeveless vest, closed down the front with a row of small buttons or hooks, and may have had a line of red piping down the front as well. This vest may have incorporated chainmail protection, as a period description of the Egyptian Mameluke battle wear is, "a suit of armour, consisting of interwoven links of steel, under their dress."[41]

Metal Helmet

A period description of the helmet worn by Egyptian Mameluke in battle is, "an open helmet"[42]; which appears as a Zirkhli helmet type, with an internal chinstrap. A considerable change occurred since the 16th and 17th Centuries, with the disappearance of the fully visored helmet, with enclosed ear and neck guards. Napoleonic Era Zirkhli helmets appear in two sets of illustrations, from 1803[43], and 1813[44]. Similar to traditional Indian-Persian helmets retaining the retractable nose guard, and chainmail Coif: neck curtain. Its most visible difference was the addition of a large ball-finial. The major change was the presence of a large set of brass chinscales and side attachment bosses fitted

33	Phillips, 1803.
34	Marsigli, 1732.
35	Sevket, 1907.
36	Marsigli, 1732.
37	Sevket, 1907.
38	Walsh, 1803.
39	Castellan, 1812.
40	Kobell, 1813.
41	McLean, 1818.
42	McLean, 1818.
43	Walsh, 1803.
44	Kobell, 1813.

to the helmets. The Zirkhli helmet likely appeared as early as 1803, around the same time that European helmet, and shako design included chinscales and bosses. Zirkhli helmet are also depicted with steel chinscales and bosses, or lacking nose guard, and fitted with brass chinscales and bosses. Modern illustrations tend to show Mameluke during Napoleon's Campaign in Egypt wearing Indian-Persian helmets with spiked-finials[45]. This type of helmet was used by earlier period Zirkhli, and distinctively Turkish versions of Indian-Persian helmets were commonly modelled with a face and horns. The explanation for a face on the front of the helmet - it represents a, "legendary powerful being known as a Deer"[46].

▶ Egyptian Khedive's Zirkhagi: Iron Men Bodyguard, from the 1830s[47], and from 1883[48], wearing latest Wilkinson Sword Company coat of mail, and gauntlets set (1860), and Birmingham helmets[49]. The 1830s Era metal helmet has European chinscales and bosses. The metal visor, and back protection resembles a lobster-tailed pot helmet. The retractable arrow nose guard and crescent finial was seen in later versions of the helmet from the Crimean War Era. Body protection consists of a long-sleeved chainmail shirt (earlier Turkish versions were short-sleeved). The 1830s Era Egyptian chainmail shirt was leather edged, and cut into large dragon's teeth. European gauntlet gloves, and black riding boots with spurs complete the dress.

C.Flaherty

---

45   Haythornthwaite, 1998.
46   Laking, 1964.
47   Unknown, 1820.
48   London Illustrated News, 1882.
49   Robinson, 1967.

The face was also called a Div: Demon:

> "In the myths recorded by the author Ferdowsi in his 10th Century work Shahnameh, the great Persian hero Rostam must complete seven labours in order to rescue his King Key Kayus, held captive by the Divs (Demons) of Mazandaran. The final of these labours is the location and slaying of Div-e-Sepid (the White Demon), who is King of all the Divs. As Herakles (known as Hercules to the Romans) wore the skin of the Nemean Lion after he had killed it, so Rostam wore the face of Div-e-Sepid on his helmet. As such, this helmet symbolically suggests that the owner possessed the heroic and awe-inspiring qualities of Rostam, much as lion-like helmets in later Centuries spoke to Europeans of the qualities of Herakles."[50]

Often early 20th Century chainmail armour from the Khevsur people in Georgia, as well as later 19th Century Indian-Persian collectable armour, are identified as Ottoman or Turkish. Such helmets were popular collectables in Britain, in the post-Omduman Period, and still appear in the collector's market as Turkish. The disparity is due mostly to the popularity of the Indian-Persian helmet in the later 19th Century, among Orientalist-collectors, which also saw large numbers of the pieces specifically manufactured for the European market.

▲ A WW1 Turkish Army Soldier's belt buckle, displaying a date from 1916, has been engraved by an artisan and depicts, inside the star and crescent badge a Div: Demon with a human face, and animal ears or horns.

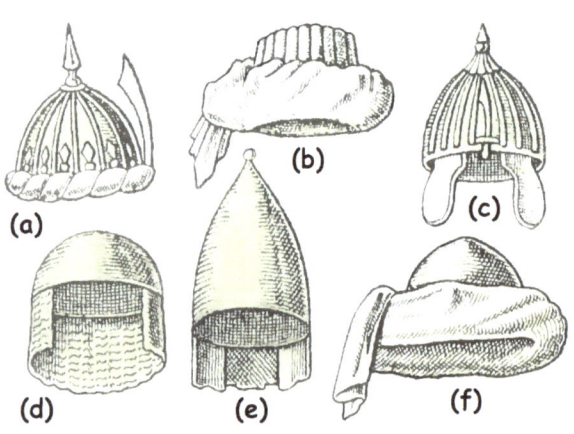

◄ Six: 1732 illustrations of metal helmets, three of which have Caouk: turbans fitted[51][52]. Rather than being decorative, the Caouk had a protective function, and were said to be so effectively constructed, that it took great skill to even cut it with a scimitar being composed of a mixture of wool and cotton, covered over with thick cloth[53]. (a) Dome metal helmet with reinforced ribs, retractable nose guard, large spike finial, and Caouk. (b) Metal helmet with nose guard, made to resemble a Cahouk: quilted top hat with Caouk. (c) Dome metal helmet with reinforced ribs, spike finial, retractable nose guard and hanging cheek plates. (d) Plain metal dome helmet with chainmail Coif: neck curtain. (e) Tall pointed plain metal helmet with hanging neck plates. (f) Plain metal dome helmet with Caouk.

50 Pitt Rivers Museum.
51 Marsigli, 1732.
52 Sevket, 1907.
53 Wittman, 1803.

UNIFORMS

Along with a metal helmet, and body armour, an illustration of a Zirkhli in, "Turkish Cavalry" that dates between 1809 till 1813[54], shows wearing an orange collarless sleeve shirt or jacket with cuffs, that end over the hands with triangular points, that can be folded-back giving the appearance of pointed cuffs. Pink Russian pants complete the dress.

FIGURE 5: Zirkhli in full Indian-Persian armour (1750 onwards). FIGURE 5a: Silahtar Regiment Soldier's helmet with Janissary plume, and spoon holder positioned to the side of the retractable nose guard.

---

54   Kobell, 1813.

FIGURE 6: Zirkhli wearing a chainmail short-sleeved shirt (1813).

CHAPTER 3: PROVINCIAL SIPAHI LIGHT CAVALRY AND LANCERS

A 1798 survey of the Turkish Army's actual strength identified some, "10,000 Paid Regulated"[55], and another 132,000 Timariot Provincial Cavalry[56]. Traditionally, a Provincial Cavalry Soldier: Timarli Sipahis [Timariot] provided their own arms and horse along with his Cebelu: Armed Retainers[57]. Provincial Sipahi Alay: Regiments were located outside Constantinople in the Provinces: "Throughout the whole Empire … the Sipahi … are spread over all the towns, and more particularly in the country-places"[58]. Composed of numerous individual Sipahi Timar fiefs, traditionally granted directly by the Sultan giving the landowner income in return for military service. Timariot Provincial Cavalry when not on active duty, were led by their Sanjakbeg: District, and Beglerbegs: Provincial Governors[59]. By end of the 17th Century, the falling number of effective Cavalry Soldiers had led to formation of the Kapuhalki: Troops of the Gate, who were maintained by Governors and local strong-men.

In 1792, Sultan Selim III had tried to create a Summer Warfare Corps drawn from Anatolian Cavalry[60]. It is generally understood, that Sultan Selim III had undertook a general reform of the Sipahi ordering registered active Horse Soldiers to come to Constantinople for instruction from Western, mostly French advisers for six months training every two years[61]. This produced a force of around 10,000 Paid Mounted Regulars, likely organized into ten Provincial Sipahi Alay of 1,000 Soldiers each. It is possible these were either trained and equipped as Light Cavalry or Lancers.

UNIFORMS

Sipahi typically wore a tall wide-topped cylindrical peakless fez-styled hat, seen in many forms during the 18th Century, and Napoleonic Era, in yellow[62], brown[63], or red colour[64]. Sipahi also typically wore a red Cahouk: quilted top hat with a white Caouk: turban[65]. A blue Cahouk with a white Caouk is also known[66]. The Cahouk had a wide-top with deep vertical lines of stitching forming pads. Commonly associated with the Sipahi, Mameluke, or higher-level Janissary Officers. An 1803 painting of Sultan Selim III in audience shows him wearing such a hat, with a white Caouk added. Behind a raised top-brim the inner hat was dome-topped[67]. The Cahouk with its turban, was made as a complete piece of formed or shaped headgear, which afforded its wearer a certain level of protection from edged weapons. For instance, an account describing Mameluke headgear, also suggests it was protected with metal: "On their heads they wore cylindrical yellow turbans, metal-circled, and wrapped round with many folds of muslin"[68]. According, to an account from Egypt in 1800, the Caouk component were so effectively constructed, that it apparently took great skill to even cut it

---

55	Eton, 1798.
56	Eton, 1798.
57	Agoston, 2011.
58	Olivier, 1801.
59	Agoston, 2011.
60	Nicolle, 1998.
61	Nicolle, 1998.
62	McLean, 1818.
63	Unknown, 1805.
64	McLean, 1818.
65	Kapidagli, 1803.
66	Unknown, 1810.
67	Brindesi, 1850.
68	Grant, 2007.

with a scimitar, famed as these were for their immensely sharp blades, as it was: "composed of a mixture of wool and cotton, covered over with thick cloth, it required no little adroitness and dexterity to penetrate into its substance by a blow of the … [scimitar]."[69]

An 1805 illustration of a Cavalleristen von Bagdad: Cavalry Soldier from Bagdad[70], shows a long buttoned yellow coat reaching down to the lower legs, that appears to have small turned-down collar over another red open long coat with short sleeves. The Soldier wears a very tall red Cahouk with a white and blue striped Caouk. Purple Russian pants and yellow European riding boots, with distinctive high heels complete the dress.

1810 PAID MOUNTED REGULARS

In the 1810 Sultan Mahmud II Grand Review[71], Sipahi Light Cavalry (which is possibly one of the Paid Mounted Regulars) is depicted, led by its Officer (wearing a badge mounted on the turban), and Alemdar: Flag Bearer Officer (under the New Order Army Regulars organization). Both Officers are shown wearing a collarless buttoned long light-blue coat, with tight-fitting long sleeves, red waist sash, red Russian pants, and red Turkish riding boots. Officers, like the rest of the Soldiers, wear red Cahouk with a white Caouk. Troopers all wear the same uniform consisting of a yellow collarless knee-length coat, with tight-fitting long sleeves, red waist sash, red Russian pants, and red Turkish riding boots.

Two group illustrations show uniformed Lancers, in the 1810 Sultan Mahmud II Grand Review[72], and among, "Turkish Cavalry", that dates between 1809 till 1813[73], and show Soldiers wearing short red jackets, some with tight-fitting long, or wide short sleeves, or sleeveless, blue Russian pants, with red low conical hats, or Cahouk with a white Caouk.

TIMARIOTE SIPAHI

Two group illustrations show various Timariote Sipahi, from the 1810 Sultan Mahmud II Grand Review[74], that have largely similar Soldier-types depicted in, "Turkish Cavalry", that dates between 1809 till 1813[75], and show two main forms of dress. Wearing blue, yellow, red, or purple bolero jackets, most are plain (but fur-edged versions are known), with short sleeves, over collarless shirts with tight-fitting long sleeves, dark-blue Russian pants, and yellow or red Turkish slipper-shoes. All the Cavalry Soldiers wear red Cahouk with a white Caouk. Officers appear to wear long collarless wrap-around coats with tight-fitting long sleeves, bound with a waist sash, mostly yellow in colour. Blue Cahouk with a white Caouk appear to be more common.

69	Wittman, 1803.
70	Unknown, 1805.
71	Unknown, 1810.
72	Unknown, 1810.
73	Kobell, 1813.
74	Unknown, 1810.
75	Kobell, 1813.

C.Flaherty

FIGURE 7: Cavalry Soldier from Bagdad, who is spear, and bow armed (1805).

21

FIGURE 8: Turkish Cavalry Soldier's lance pennant (1817). A green lance pennant with a white crescent was particularly identified with the Dey of Algiers.
FIGURE 9: Paid Mounted Regulars Lancer (1810).
FIGURE 10: Sipahi Soldier's lance pennant.

FIGURE 11: Timariote Sipahi Soldier (1810).

CHAPTER 4: DELI

The Deli [Delhi; Deliler] Cavalry were classed as volunteers, and are described, "[as] … the most numerous and famed of this adventurous tribe"[76]. Some historians suggest Deli were a specific name for a Regiment[77][78]. However, the more likely explanation is that Deli was a granted title[79][80]. The Deli Cavalry was described in 1800, by an English Diplomat:

> "The … [name: Deli] … signifies madmen, is well applied to them: they form a Light Cavalry, and boast of never refusing to undertake the most hazardous enterprises: they are the enfans perdus … [terrible children] … of the Turkish Army"[81].

A similar allusion was used in an 1803 account from Egypt, similarly, commenting that in the Turkish Army, the Deli,

> "whose name implies desperadoes, or madmen, form a part of the Light Cavalry. They boast, not without reason, of their courage and temerity; and are said to feel no hesitation in undertaking the most daring enterprises."[82]

Daring to do acts not normally expected of Soldiers, and thus sought to constantly prove themselves in battle, which may account for their status as volunteers, even though these were Regular Soldiers in the Provincial Sipahi Alay. It is known, to become a Deli, a Cavalry Soldier had to have been victorious against eight, or ten mounted Warriors[83]. This may refer to victories achieved during battles, or at the Djerrid: mounted stick-fighting contest. Even though it may have been the case, that there were no actual Deli Regiments, named as such, it is known that the Deli component of the Cavalry sent to Egypt in 1800, were described as the, "most numerous" of the 25,000 in this force[84]. It may well have been the case, that larger formations of Deli were specifically banded together on an ad hoc basis without any formal organization.

DELI CAVALRY ORIGIN

Deli Cavalry origin can be traced back to the 16th Century Turkish Governors of Bosnia and Semendire, who founded special frontier Light Cavalry units:

> "At the same time … [alongside the Akinci] … Governors founded a totally new kind of frontier light Cavalry unit, called Deli (daredevil or literally 'crazy'), as their personal retinues. The Bosnian and Semendire Governors created the first … [Deli] … the leader most associated with these troops was the Bosnian Governor … Husrevbegova, who employed about 10,000 of them so effectively that other frontier and inland district … [Sanjakbeg: Governors] … of Rumelia … [Ottoman South-Eastern Europe] … began to imitate him … The … [Deli] … were a totally different type of … Soldier. Most of them were recent converts to Islam (usually from Bosnian, Serb, and Croat origins) and were fanatically dedicated to wage

---

76   Morier, 1801.
77   Goodwin, 1998.
78   Turnbull, 2003.
79   Mallet, 1684.
80   Goffman, 2002.
81   Morier, 1801.
82   Wittman, 1803.
83   Chalcondyles, 1662.
84   Morier, 1801.

war against infidels. They wore exaggerated and wild costumes as uniforms, which were a mixture of furs and feathers of animals of prey. Their weapons also looked terrifying with exaggerated features and accessories. However, all these served a very important purpose, which was to terrify the enemy … Moreover, in addition to their raiding potential, they … turned out to be more useful … in conventional military duties due to their superior command, control, and organizational structure."[85]

Deli Cavalry were enrolled in units under various Vilayet: Turkish Provincial Governorships, as Personal Guard Cavalry for the Rumelia: Ottoman South-Eastern Europe Beglerbegs: Senior or Province Governors.

DELI ORGANIZATION

Basic Deli organization consisted of 50 to 60 Mounted Soldiers formed under the banner of a Delibasi: Head Mad-Head. Deli were known subject to strict discipline under their Commanders. The common historical view is that the Deli Cavalry were abolished in 1791[86]; however, the terminology was still being employed in the Napoleonic Era[87].

UNIFORMS

Famed for their tradition of exaggerated and wild costumes as uniforms, wearing furs and feathers representing various predator animals. There are several descriptions of the Deli uniform, namely, "they dress like the … [Turkish] … but are distinguished by a hollow cap of sheep's skin, made in the form of a cylinder, and tied about the head with a … [handkerchief]."[88] It is known that these tall hats were called a, "Tarturas"[89]. It is also known, that this was a: "very high cap of a cylindrical form, made of pasteboard, and covered either with sheep skin died of a black colour, or with black cloth. This cap is secured to the head by a coloured muslin or cotton handkerchief."[90] Identical headgear was worn by the Humbaraci: Mortar Troops.
An 1803 illustration of a Deli Cavalry Soldier from Napoleon's Campaign in Egypt[91][92], shows them wearing a black Tarturas hat with a dark-green turban, and a dark-green wrap-around short jacket with broad lapels and long tight-fitting sleeves. Brown pants, white waist sash and red Turkish riding boots complete the dress. An 1805 dated illustration of a Deli Cavalry Soldier from the Aleppo Vilayet: Province Governorship[93], shows them wearing a brown Tarturas hat, and long red buttoned collarless long-sleeved coat, with a yellow folded-down collar, and yellow European riding boots, with distinctive high heels, completing the dress. A later 1907 illustration[94], shows the Deli Cavalry Soldier with a light-pink Tarturas hat, with a yellow turban, and a light-green-yellow wrap-around short jacket with broad lapels and long tight-fitting sleeves. Pink pants, yellow waist sash and red Turkish riding boots complete the dress.

85	Uyar, 2009.
86	Buyukakca, 2007.
87	Phillips, 1803.
88	Morier, 1801.
89	Tyrrell, 1910.
90	Wittman, 1803.
91	Phillips, 1803,
92	Wittman, 1803.
93	Unknown, 1805.
94	Sevket, 1907.

FIGURE 12: Deli Cavalry Soldier (1803).

FIGURE 13: Deli Cavalry Soldier from the Aleppo Vilayet: Province Governorship, with small arm shield face, and bow case details (1805).

CHAPTER 5: TOPRACLY AND MOUNTED INFANTRY

A Soldier depicted with a tall conical hat, bound to the top with tightly bound patterned cloth coils, is variously described in several sources as a Sipahi[95], or Sipahi Timariote[96]. An identical illustration, dated 1802, describes this inconclusively as, "a … [Sipahi] … belonging to one of the Asiatic Provinces".[97] Identically uniformed Soldiers are seen parading as, "Turkish Infantry"[98]. The parade line of Soldiers is depicted using a large green over red swallow-tailed flag decorated with four gold crescents and the split Zulfiqar sword. The same flag is illustrated in 1907[99], and earlier in 1732, and specifically identified as being used by the Topracly: Cavalry[100]. Also called Toprakli: Territorial Cavalry[101], they have been argued to have been a type of Infantry garrisoning a Border Territory Timar Garrison, or a Sipahi Base, that were permanently fortified[102]. This appears to suggest that these Topracly may have been Dragoon Mounted Infantry. Topracly Soldier, in addition to their unique headdress, which appears to be an extremely tall red fez, bound in a zig-zag pattern of red-green-white lines, are shown wearing a white and yellow collarless undershirt, with a light-blue edged with yellow tape waist coat, under a red bolero jacket with long close-fitting sleeves with cuffs, that end over the hands with triangular points, that can be folded-back giving the appearance of pointed cuffs. Light-blue (other illustrations show dark-blue) Russian pants, and red Turkish riding boots complete the dress.

MOUNTED INFANTRY

In the 16th and 17th Centuries, Damascus Janissary were horse mounted on the march. Known as the second of the New Order Army Regiments, the Uskudar, are described as, "[a] … Provincial Militaria of Mounted Infantry"[103]. It was the case, only half the Regiment was trained as, "Cavalry so they could return to form the local Militias of the Provincial Governors and district notables … [namely the Sanjakbeg: Governor]."[104] The Uskudar Regiment uniform, "was given the color light blue for its jackets and breeches"[105]. An illustration of a, "Soldier of the Ottoman Experimental Infantry, around 1802"[106][107]; also known as: "Nefer, Soldat des Nizam Djedyd": Soldier of the New Order Army[108], shows a blue collarless bolero jacket, with double sleeves, the other sleeves hanging from the back of the shoulders. Blue Russian pants, secured with plain blue leggings with a row of buttons connecting the backs. The Soldier also wears a red waist sash, red bonnet, with a top tuft, combined with a colored fringed shawl wrapped around it. Red Turkish slipper shoes complete the dress.

95	McLean, 1818.
96	Sevket, 1907.
97	Dalvimart, 1802.
98	Kobell, 1813.
99	Sevket, 1907.
100	Marsigli, 1732.
101	Tyrrell, 1910.
102	Kolcak, 2012.
103	Nicolle, 1998.
104	Shaw, 1965.
105	Shaw, 1965.
106	Dalvimart, 1802.
107	Roubicek, 1978.
108	Castellan, 1812.

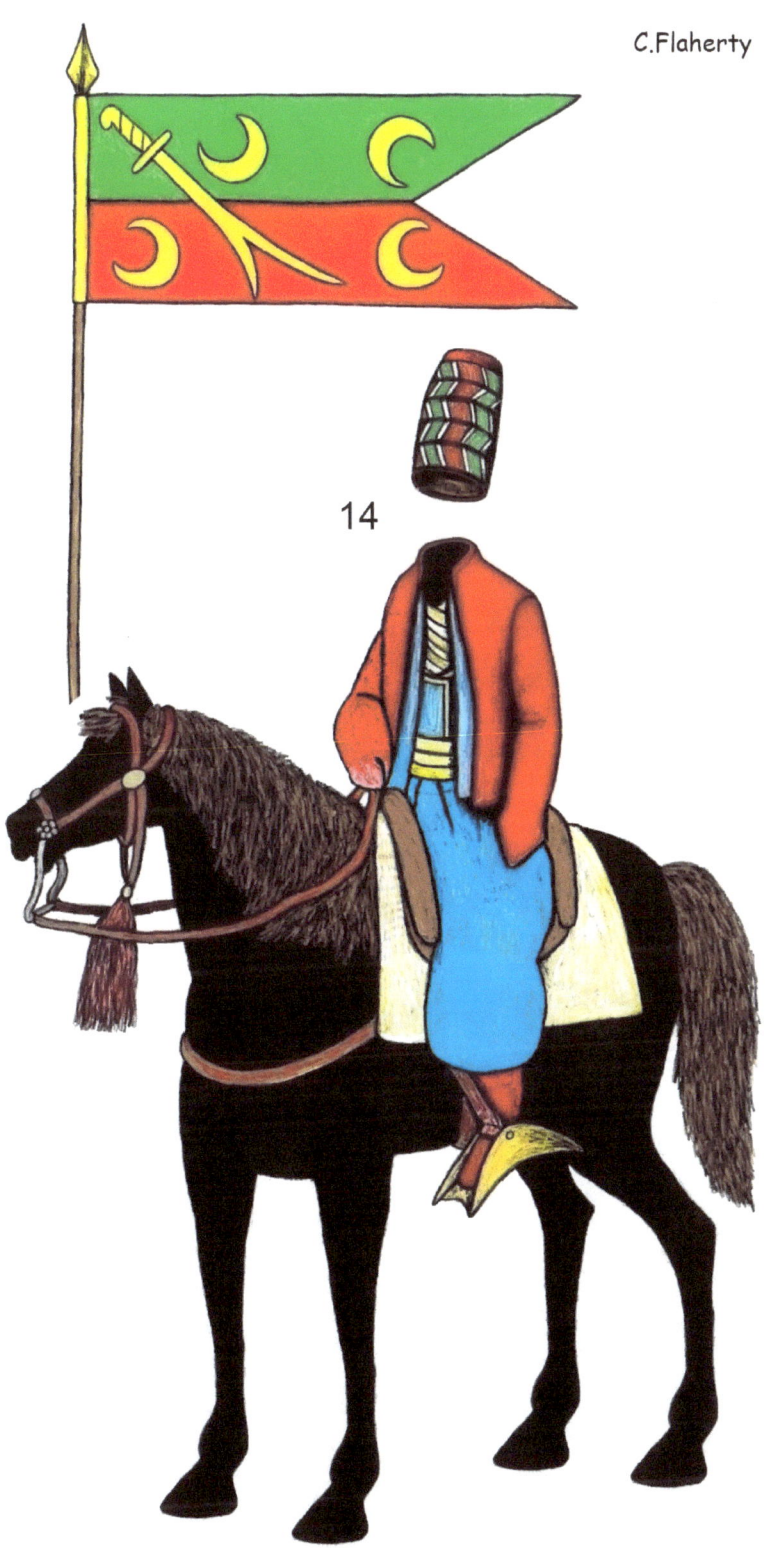

FIGURE 14: Topracly Soldier.

FIGURE 15: Uskudar Barracks Trained Mounted Infantry, and calf leggings details (1802), and Mounted Soldier's cartridge box (1810).

CHAPTER 6: MAMELUKE

Mameluke constituted their own Military Order, much like Janissary, and similarly enrolled its members for life to receive wages by the State. The uniform, consisted of broad red Russian pants (in the case of the Janissary uniform it consisted of three items: Bork: hat, breeches, and boot color). Traditionally, a Chief governed the Mameluke under whom there were twenty-four Mameluke-Bey[109]. It is known, "approximately 12,000 … [Mameluke were] … serving in Egypt at the time of the French invasion."[110][111] This description is not entirely accurate. At the time of Napoleon's invasion of Egypt many Mameluke were employed outside the Province, in three Regiments: "Mameluke of Constantinople"; the, "Mameluke of Grand Seignior … [Sultan]"; and the, "Mameluke of the Grand Vizier"[112]. More, were likely infirmed, or no longer militarily active and living in the households of their respective Bey (as was similarly practiced in Janissary Barracks). Still more were living individually within various villages ceded to them as Vassals to their Bey. It is known that the French encountered not more than 6,000 mounted Mameluke by the time of the Battle of the Pyramids (Embabeh), in 1798.

OFFICERS

Each Mameluke-Bey was also an Alay Bey – commanding their own Alay: Regiment of Mameluke[113]. Mameluke Alay were less standardized than the Provincial Sipahi, and likely fielded less than 500 mounted Warriors. However, some units were much larger: "The power and influence of the … [Bey] … were proportionate to the number of … [Mameluke] … that composed their household."[114] For instance, during Napoleon's Campaign in Egypt, the Mameluke Alay of Ibrahim-Bey had 1,200 Soldiers. Less prestigious Bey may have only had a few hundred Mameluke in their household forming their Alay. A lower graded Kiachefs [Cashefs]: Sub-Commander, whose employ was subordinate to that of a Bey was known[115]. The Vassal-Lords governed five or six villages within the district of their Master[116]. There was also an Inferior Officer called: Gindees[117].

An 1818 illustration of a Mameluke-Bey[118], shows them dressed similarly to other high-ranking Janissary Officers, wearing a long red open coat, edged with fur and three pairs of button cords over the chest, with wide sleeves that have wide opened buttoned cuff slashes, along with a long white under gown, under a patterned overshirt, with a patterned waist sash. The headgear is a tall yellow wide-topped cylindrical peakless fez-styled hat, with a white Caouk: turban secured by a wide gold tasseled tie displayed over the brow of the hat. Wide red Russian pants, and red Turkish slipper-shoes complete the dress.

An 1818 illustration of a Mameluke Officer is also known shown wearing a tall tapering red fez-styled peakless hat with a white Caouk[119]. A red long coat with wide sleeves, and blue long shirt, patterned waist sash, and yellow Turkish riding boots complete the dress. The Officer carries a boar-

---

109	Walsh, 1803.
110	Johnson, 1988.
111	McLean, 1818.
112	McLean, 1818.
113	Ozturk, 2016.
114	Walsh, 1803.
115	Walsh, 1803.
116	Morier, 1801.
117	Morier, 1801.
118	McLean, 1818.
119	McLean, 1818.

spear, like Tatar Officers carried[120]. The boar-spear weapon is nearly identical to a Napoleonic Era British Infantry Sergeant's spontoon.

STANDARDS

The Tug: horse-tail standards were commonly carried for each Mameluke-Bey. It is likely, that various Mameluke-Bey were holders of one, or two horse-tails standards. The Turkish Governor of the Egyptian Province was a holder of a three horse-tails standard. A surviving Tug: taken at the Battle of the Pyramids (Embabeh), in 1798[121], consists of a tall pole surmounted with a large highly decorated and patterned silver finial, bearing Turkish script, over a fall of red cords, topping a woven section, of yellow and red cord-work that secured the horse tail to the pole, From the fall of red cords, hung two decorative plaited long cords. A Pasha was only entitled to display their Tug standard, as a symbol of military authority during a campaign. There was no set pattern for the finial used on horse-tail standards. Illustrations show a wide number of designs for the finials or ornaments, depending on individual taste and traditions[122]. Examples are known with elaborate boar-tusk tops, or incorporating an elaborate series of coloured pom-poms and tufts at the top of the standard[123][124][125]. A large rectangular flag with dark-green, yellow and dark-green bars, is described as the, "Mamelik" Naval flag is known from a 1783 (or 1801) dated illustration[126]. This flag is likely related to the Nile Gunboat Flotilla Headquartered in Alexandria, that was led by its Mameluke Officers.

UNIFORMS

Mameluke were legendary for their colourful dress, one account describes them, "with all the luxury the country can afford, dressed in fine silk robes, fitter for a court than a camp"[127]. A description of Ibrahim-Bey's Mameluke Alay in Egypt noted, "every individual … [was] … richly dressed"[128]. Notwithstanding, this is more likely describing Ibrahim-Bey and his other Officers. Modern illustrations of Napoleonic Era Mameluke typically show them wearing Indian-Persian armour[129]. However, contemporary illustrations and descriptions indicate an altogether different appearance, and possibly suggest that the Mameluke uniform was wearing large crimson drawers; rather like the Janissary uniform was the wearing of blue breeches. The broad bloomer pants were extremely full-cut, to the point that large extra-folds of lose fabric collected between the leg holes. The leg holes were edged in tape, possibly to hold a draw string, to close the holes around the ankles. French accounts from the first battles with the Mameluke also describe: "Their costumes are brilliantly colourful; their turbans are surmounted by aigret feathers, and some wear gilded helmets."[130] This description may likely be focusing on the high-status Mameluke-Bey, and other Officers like the Kiachefs [Cashefs], or Gindees.

A modern illustration of a Mameluke in French service in 1801, in France during the First Consulate[131], show how, on first arriving Mameluke wore their Egyptian clothing, consisting of the Turkish

---

120 Williams, 2013.
121 Musee de l'Armee, 1798.
122 Vorstellung Uber der Kriegswesen, 1800.
123 Kunsthistorische Museum.
124 Nicolle, 1995.
125 Badisches Landesmuseum.
126 Bowles, 1801.
127 Low, 1911.
128 Walsh, 1803.
129 Haythornthwaite, 1998.
130 Herold, 1962.
131 Haythornthwaite, 1998.

Yelek: short waist-length coat, worn open over the waist sash. Which can be seen worn by other Napoleonic Era Sipahi. This coat had short wide sleeves, and was fur trimmed. A wrap-around Turkish shirt, which left the upper chest and neck exposed was also worn. Another style of shirt worn was cut round at the neck, and collarless. It should be noted that one of the first alterations to 'Turkish dress' in France in this period, was when Napoleon issued a decree dictating that the Mameluke Cahouk: quilted top hat should be green, beginning evolution into the French uniform of the Orient. Mameluke on their arrival in France used long-pointed blue (French Light Cavalry-styled) Schabracke with long end tassels, along with ornated Arab horse bridles.

▼ Mameluke in French service in 1801, during the First Consulate, on first arriving in France (reconstruction by the author).

▲ Mameluke in France during the First Consulate in the French uniform of the Orient.

▼ Mameluke Light Cavalry, and Zirkhli[132].

MAMELUKE ZIRKHLI

An 1803 illustration of a Zirkhli, wearing a green, with red trimmed cloth covered sleeveless chainmail over-vest, is also identified as a Mameluke in Egypt[133], shows yellow and white striped wide sleeved shirt, with wide red Russian pants and yellow Turkish riding boots. Another illustration showing a Zirkhli, identifiable by the helmet, wearing a green and white striped overcoat among a group of, "Turkish Cavalry" that dates between 1809 till 1813[134], is commonly associated with troops from Egypt at this time[135]. Another Zirkhli in the group shows a red close-fitting sleeved shirt, and wide red Russian pants. The body armour in this instance consists of a chainmail short-sleeved shirt.

132   Castellan, 1812.
133   Walsh, 1803.
134   Kobell, 1813.
135   Haythornthwaite, 1998.

MAMELUKE LIGHT CAVALRY

A description of the Mameluke of Egypt:

> "The dress constantly worn by the inferior ... [Mameluke] ... was a pair of large crimson drawers of thick Venetian cloth attached to slippers of red leather, and a greenish cap of a peculiar form, fancifully decorated with a turban."[136]

An 1803 illustration of a Mameluke Light Cavalry Soldier shows wearing a very tall red (brown in some versions) and extremely tapered tall wide-topped peakless fez-styled hat with a white Caouk[137]. The Mameluke wears a yellow, possibly black striped wide sleeved shirt, with a high-cut green bolero jacket, with brown fur edging, with short wide sleeves. Wide red Russian pants, and red Turkish riding boots complete the dress. Another 1803 illustration of a Mameluke Light Cavalry Soldier shows wearing a short green waist jacket closed at the front, with gold trim, broad red Russian pants, a white cloth wrap-around turban and yellow Turkish riding boots completing the dress. An 1812 illustration of a Mameluke Light Cavalry Soldier[138], shows them wearing a green close-fitting sleeved shirt, with a high-cut yellow bolero jacket with short wide sleeves. A green waist band, and wide red Russian pants, and yellow Turkish slipper-shoes. A low red skull cap and pink turban complete the dress. An 1818 illustration of a, "Mameluke of Egypt"[139], shows a large red cloth wrap-around turban, a white wide sleeve shirt, a collarless, brown sleeveless coat, closed with some small brass ball buttons, a large gold waist sash with a fringed end, large red Russian pants, and yellow Turkish slipper-shoes completing the dress.

Constantinople Mameluke Light Cavalry Alay

An 1818 illustration of, "Mameluke of Grand Seignior… [Sultan]" suggest, this Alay like the two other Constantinople based Mameluke were largely Light Cavalry, as the Soldier is shown wearing a white collarless shirt with long close-fitting sleeves under a light-blue short-sleeved bolero jacket edged with white tape. A red cloth wrap-around turban, red waist sash, and yellow Turkish slipper-shoes complete the dress. Oddly despite being a Mameluke, white and not red Russian pants are depicted. The second 1818 illustration of the, "Mameluke of the Grand Vizier"[140], shows this Soldier wearing a chest-high light-blue vest with white tape stripes, and white long wide sleeves, under a loosely-fitting open red jacket with short shoulder covering sleeves. A broad yellow waist sash, yellow Turkish slipper-shoes, and loose red bonnet with yellow cloth wrap-around turban complete the dress. Despite being a Mameluke broad dark-blue Russian pants are worn. The third 1818 illustration of, "Mameluke of Constantinople", only shows a Soldier from the back-view, wearing an orange collarless shirt with long close-fitting sleeves, under a light-blue sleeveless long coat, with shoulder wings, and black tape edging. Yellow Turkish riding boots, red fez, and white cloth wrap-around turban complete the dress.

MAMELUKE CAMELEERS AND FOOT SERVANTS-AT-ARMS

During Napoleon's Campaign in Egypt, a force of Mameluke under Ibrahim-Bay that had survived the Battle of the Pyramids (Embabeh), in 1798, went on to join the British and Turkish Armies, operating against the French. It appears to have been a conventional sized unit, as about 1,200 Soldiers

---

136	McLean, 1818.
137	Walsh, 1803.
138	Castellan, 1812.
139	McLean, 1818.
140	McLean, 1818.

are usually mentioned in campaign memoirs[141][142]. It included a sub-unit of Cameleers (Division Wing), "mounted on those running camels or dromedaries"[143]. Like Mameluke horse equipment, Cameleers' saddlery was equally impressive: "red velvet saddles and silver rings in the noses of their camels and with silk cords to guide them"[144]. An eye-witness account described how the Foot Servants-at-Arms ran after each Mameluke Cameleer:

> "Each of them has an Arab or two running in the rear on foot carrying lances which they throw with great dexterity from their camels or dromedaries, and are sure of their object at 30- or 40-yards distance"[145].

It was said that every mounted Mameluke was, "attended by a servant on foot, carrying a long stick in his hand."[146] Mameluke Foot Servants-at-Arms, primary function, was to:

> "simply to mop up after the charge, finishing off any survivors and retrieving the firearms discarded by their masters during the charge. The ratio of servants to … [Mameluke] … was approximately two to one."[147]

Mameluke Foot Servants-at-Arms were Fellahim [Fellahs]: Local Village Peasants, and constituted a permanent force of trained Warriors making up the bulk of the Mameluke's Foot Troops that accompanied the Cavalry[148]. It is known they, "dressed in their traditional costume of flowing white robes and turbans"[149]. An 1803 illustration shows yellow slipper shoes, off-white cloak-cloth wrapped around the body, with much of the chest exposed, and off-white cloth wrap-around turban[150].

TACTICS

Mameluke, "taken as Light Troops, or as individual horsemen, are … without tactics, and never acting in a body"[151]. Mameluke practiced one battlefield tactic: a full charge, adopting a long line, or possibly double-line formation said to have been formed into a crescent. This was preceded by single or small groups of Mameluke scouting ahead looking for weaknesses to attack. Mameluke were equipped as Zirkhli, Light Cavalry, or Cameleers with their Foot Servants-at-Arms and may have attacked in various groups according to their particular skills and training. Accounts also record individual Mameluke ambushing French Soldiers on the march[152].

WEAPONS

Individual Mameluke carried many weapons: "sabres, lances, maces, spears, rifles, battle axes, and daggers, and each has three pairs of pistols"[153].

141	Morier, 1801.
142	Alison, 1842.
143	Low, 1911.
144	Low, 1911.
145	Low, 1911.
146	Walsh, 1803.
147	Johnson, 1988.
148	McNabb, 2017.
149	Johnson, 1988.
150	Walsh, 1803.
151	Walsh, 1803.
152	Scott, 1827.
153	Herold, 1962.

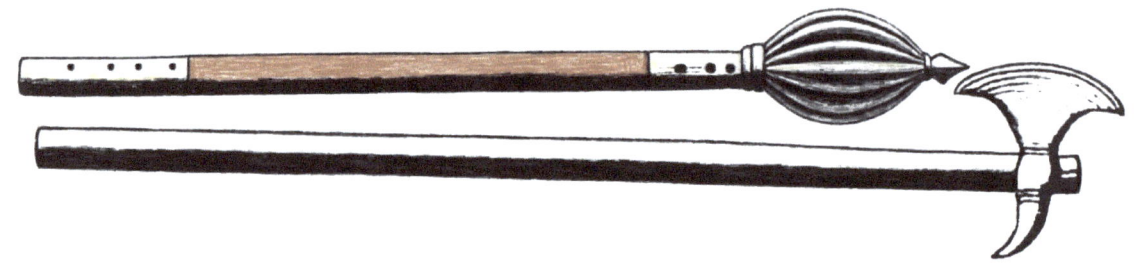

▲ A 1732 illustration of a Turkish Topuz [Gurz]: mace, and battle axe used as a Cavalry weapon[154].

A small brown leather, with a wide grey metal rimmed arm shield is depicted in an 1803 illustration[155]. It is known that Mameluke, "trained from their infancy to military evolutions, and display astonishing skill in the exercise of the javelin."[156] The most distinguishing feature of Mameluke Officers was the valuable weapons they carried; one report, "his … sword, and pistols, beautifully wrought and inlaid with silver, are worth very great sums"[157]. An 1812 illustration of a Mameluke Light Cavalry Soldier depicts a large yellow leather pistol holster slung over the front of the saddle[158].

HORSE BRIDLES, FURNITURE AND SCHABRACKE

Ordinary Mameluke horse bridles, furniture and Schabracke appear similar to Sipahi versions. The main difference is rather than square saddle cloths, Mameluke versions flange-outwards on either side, and have broad white and colored (red and blue) striped boarders[159]. The horse harness chest strap appears to have been more substantial, as well displaying a large gold metal flower badge. Descriptions of the rich and expensive horse equipment, with head harness with long-thick forelock knotted tassels, and tassels hanging about, are well known[160], which likely belonged to Officers: "The magnificence of the trappings, with which … [horses] … are covered, is amazing, and the saddles and housings glitter with gold and silver, almost dazzling the eyes of the astonished spectator."[161] A surviving gilded metal and enameled Mameluke horse bridle and Schabracke, taken at the Battle of the Pyramids (Embabeh), in 1798, covers the entire body of the horse[162].

154	Marsigli, 1732.
155	Walsh, 1803.
156	McLean, 1818.
157	Walsh, 1803.
158	Castellan, 1812.
159	Walsh, 1803.
160	Brouillet, 1961.
161	Walsh, 1803.
162	Musee de l'Armee, 1798.

FIGURE 16: Mameluke-Bey (1818). FIGURE 16a: Mameluke Bey's Tug: horse-tail standard (1800).

FIGURE 17: Mamelik Naval flag. Mameluke Officer's flag, Nile Gunboat Flotilla Headquartered in Alexandria (1783 or 1801).

FIGURE 18: Gilded metal and enameled Mameluke horse bridle and Schabracke, taken at the Battle of the Pyramids (Embabeh), in 1798.

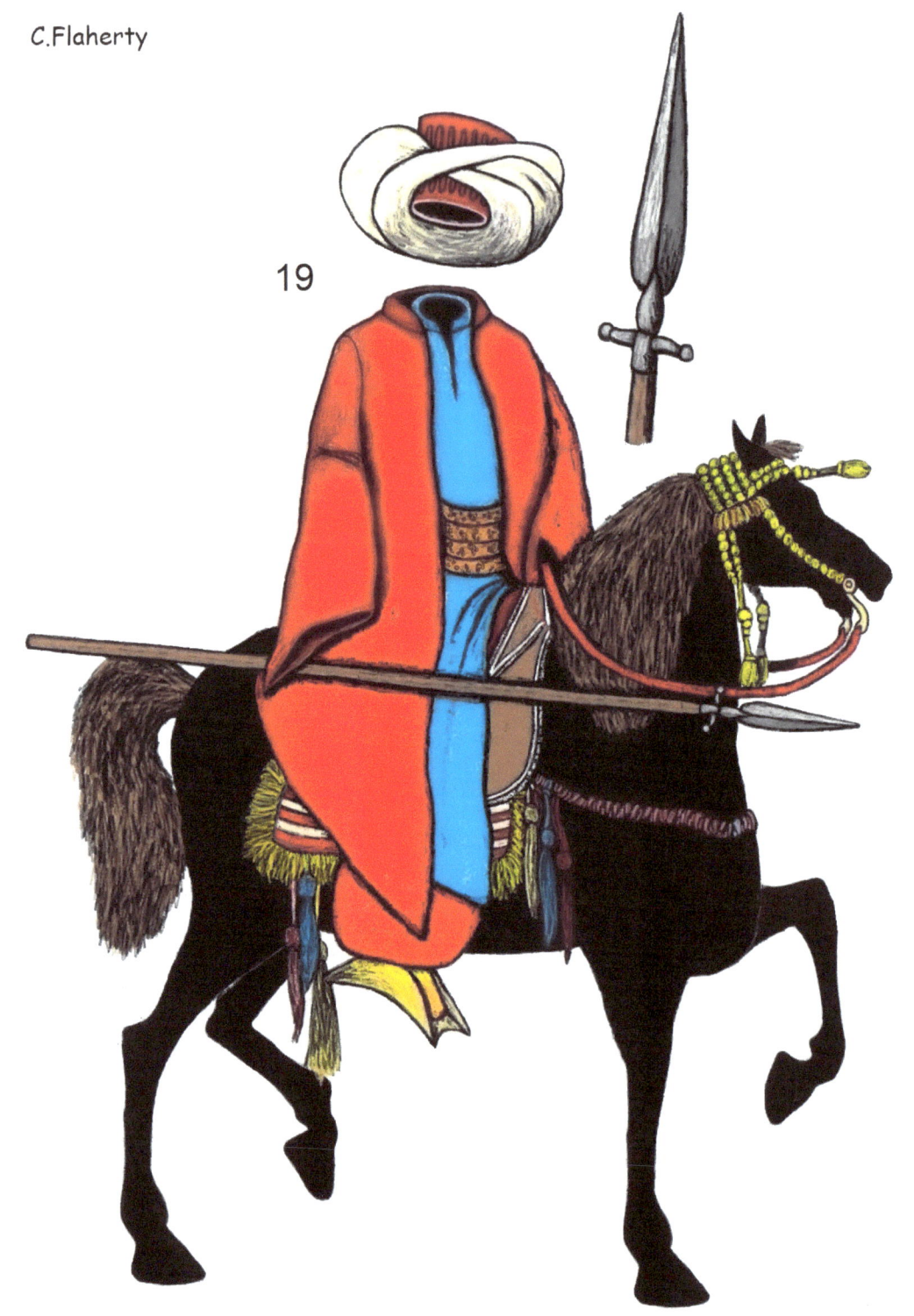

FIGURE 19: Mameluke Officer, with boar-spear details.

FIGURE 20: Mameluke Zirkhli wearing striped overcoat associated with Egyptian troops (1813).

FIGURE 21: Mameluke Zirkhli (1800).

FIGURE 22: Mameluke Zirkhli, shield and Kilij broad sword (1800).

FIGURE 23: Mameluke Cameleer's Accompanying Foot Soldier in Egypt (1800).
FIGURE 24: Mameluke Cameleer in Egypt (1800).

FIGURE 25: Mameluke Light Cavalry Soldier in Egypt, with small arm shield face details (1800).

FIGURE 26: Mameluke Light Cavalry Soldier in Egypt (around 1818).

FIGURE 27: Mameluke of Constantinople around 1818 (author's reconstruction).

CHAPTER 7: BEDOUIN

In the Napoleonic Era, desert nomadic Bedouin (also commonly called: Bedoween), or Bedouin-Arabs, even the name - Berber, is often used, in Egypt were raised to form Mounted Tribal Troops. Some three thousand Arab Horse Soldiers were usually employed by the Dey of Algiers, and by the Bey of each Province to accompany detachments of Janissary responsible for collecting taxes. Outside North Africa, and Egypt, many Arab, and Bedouin Light Cavalry were employed throughout the Empire. The formal role in the Turkish military, as the 'Arab Cavalry' was to emerge much later in the post-Crimean War. In the late 18th Century, in Syria, there is mention of large units, of 300 to 1,000 Egyptian Bedouin Cavalry being employed by the Turkish Governor[163]. Known to come from specific tribes – the Hawwara, and the Hinadi; the various unit sizes reflected the organization of the Bedouin, "they ... are formed into large and small tribes."[164] Several illustration depicting an Arab-Bedouin Scheck [Sheik]: Chief[165][166], are known, they led their own Tribal Regiments, as Hereditary Lords. Described as a, "Military Chief of Upper Egypt"[167], the Officer wears yellow Turkish slipper-shoes, with loose white pants that only come down to the knees (the lower leg is bare), and a buttoned white shirt with broad blue waist sash. A buttoned red waistcoat, with yellow piping, and blue and white loosely wrapped turban around a low grey coloured fez completes the dress.

DRESS

Bedouin dress in Egypt during the Napoleonic invasion was described as, "very light, consisting of nothing more than a loose frock and a turban"[168]. It is known a tall wicker brimless hat (to keep the head cool), was worn covered with a large keffiyeh, with long silk covered, cotton stuffed sausage coiled around, or cloth forming a turban to protect against blade weapons. A white long shirt, that could also be blue, reflecting Bedouin may have occasionally use the same clothing as other Egyptian Fellahim: Villagers, which accounts describe them wearing a long blue cotton shirt hanging loose to the heels[169]. Blue long shirts did become the basis of the French raised troop of Guides Indigene (1799 till 1801), which was modified, with the addition of green collar and cuffs - giving it a European military uniform appearance[170]. An 1840 illustration of a Kabyle: a Berber Infantry Soldier of Algeria or Tunisia[171], shows similarity to an 1800 dated illustration of a Soldat Egyptien: Egyptian Soldier[172]. Both illustrations share some similarity with descriptions of the Bedouin Warrior; such as wearing long white loose-fitting shirts. An 1803 dated illustration of a Bedoween [Bedouin] -Arab, shows a Foot-Fighting Warrior[173], which is similar to an 1802 dated illustration of a Bedouin–Arab Warrior[174], it depicts a bare Soldier only wearing a wrap-around off-white cloak-cloth, exposing the chest, except for a portion of loose cloth covering the neck and shoulders, an off-white head wrap and yellow Turkish slipper-shoes completing the dress.

163	Douwes, 2000.
164	Morier, 1801.
165	Dalvimart, 1802.
166	McLean, 1818.
167	McLean, 1818.
168	Walsh, 1803.
169	Morier, 1801.
170	Knotel, 1963.
171	Rigo, 1840.
172	Unknown, 1800.
173	Walsh, 1803.
174	Dalvimart, 1802.

WEAPONS

A description of the Bedouin Warrior states: "[their] … weapons are a long gun and a dagger."[175] A period description adds more details about the weapons used: "Their arms consist of a musket with matchlock slung round the arm, a sabre, and a long spear, which they carry in the hand."[176] While another description, states: "arms … [of the Bedouin] … consist of a musket, provided with a match-lock, slung round the arm, a sabre, and a long spear, which they carry in the hand. The latter of these weapons they employ with great effect, when in pursuit of an enemy."[177] Called an Az-zagayah: hunting and fishing spear or lance[178]. Commonly very long (up to 14 feet or more), with bamboo shafts and often fitted with long metal multi-pronged heads. Arab hunting and fishing spears remained unchanged till modern times and were used in battle by Mounted Arab Warriors. An 1850 to 1856 illustration of an, "Arab sentry of the Turkish Irregular Army", shows equipped with a hunting and fishing spear being used as a weapon[179]. Some 60 years later, in a WW1 photograph of Arab Cavalry the same type of spears can be seen, erroneously identified as, "military issue heavy lances"[180]. A yellow (possibly cane woven) cartridge box slung on a carry strap is depicted worn by a Berber Infantry Soldier in Algeria or Tunisia, from around 1800 to 1809[181]. An 1803 illustration of a Bedouin Warrior shows wearing a rectangular box with semi-rounded sides, on a broad red carry strap[182]. An 1802 dated illustration of a Bedouin–Arab Warrior shows slung on a thin red strap a large red box, with rounded sides[183].

WARFARE AND TACTICS

Bedouin Warriors' are described, "mounted on horseback … [and] … all furnished with horses, capable of undergoing the greatest fatigue in their excursions over the deserts"[184]. The warfare of the Bedouin is described as, "predatory incursions", and these people live, "by continual pillage and warfare."[185] A description of their mounted-attacks: "for their long spears and their swift mares give them the advantage when they become the pursuers"[186]. Another description, states:

> "Notwithstanding they are themselves armed with muskets, they have a great dread of firearms, and abandon the field to their adversary, as soon as a few of their party are brought down by the balls. They cannot, therefore, be deemed formidable, when opposed to troops subjected to any degree of discipline; and are only so when they encounter an unprepared enemy, or one greatly inferior in force."[187]

Bedouin Warriors are described as mounted; however, period illustrations depict them as foot fighters[188][189][190][191].

175	Walsh, 1803.
176	Morier, 1801.
177	Wittman, 1803.
178	Eric, 1914.
179	Valfrio, 1856.
180	Uyar, 2009
181	Rigo, 1840.
182	Walsh, 1803.
183	Dalvimart, 1802.
184	Walsh, 1803.
185	Walsh, 1803.
186	Morier, 1801.
187	Wittman, 1803.
188	Unknown, 1800.
189	Dalvimart, 1802.
190	Walsh, 1803.
191	Rigo, 1840.

WAR CAMELS

War camels used by the Bedouin were recorded in a 1798 French account of the Battle of Chebreisse [Shubra-Khit; Chobrakit], in Egypt recalls seeing Bedouin Warriors mounted on camels firing their small saddle mounted cannons[192]. The cannon were likely identical weapons to the Persian Zamburechki, or Musquetooners (large-bore cannon-muskets).

FIGURE 28: Bedouin war camel in Egypt (1800).

---

192   Strathern, 2008.

FIGURE 29: Bedouin–Arab Cavalry (1802).

FIGURE 30: Military Chief of Upper Egypt.

CHAPTER 8: TATAR

Almost every Tatar had a horse and arms of their own, and formed a body of Auxiliary Cavalry, for the Turkish[193]. There was also the Seimans: Regiment of 1,600 Mounted Troops, sent from Constantinople, and paid for by the Sultan as a Personal Guard for the Khan[194]. The Tatar Army in the autumn of 1777, "[was] … forty thousand … all well mounted and armed."[195] A major change in the organization of the Tatar, occurred with Russian annexation of the Khanate in 1783. Loss of the Khanate impacted the Turkish military, "the Turks were formerly assisted by numerous hordes of Tatar … this supply is now cut off by their cession of the Tatar Provinces to the … Russian Empress"[196]. After 1783, the Tatar may have organizationally split, and operated under different Khan. It is known, when they were with the main Army under the Grand Vizier: "A certain number of these Tatar, under a Khan, or Chief of their own nation … [were used]"[197]. Around the late 1790s, it is known that some three hundred Tatar Princes had Chifflick: country house farming estates granted to them by the Sultan between Constantinople and Adrianople[198]. Large numbers of Tatar fled resettling in Ottoman-Dobruca, a territory forming part of Bulgaria and Romania, and the Tatar there continued in their Light Cavalry roles, such as patrolling, and skirmishing, "[and] … were organized into Provisional Military Units by the … authorities."[199] Tatar of Circassia (a region in the North Caucasus and along the northeast shore of the Black Sea), appear to have continued in their traditional role as Vanguard Troops of the Turkish Army[200], which was also a Light Cavalry function. A 16th Century miniature painting of the Tatar Advance Guard shows a large yellow triangle shaped flag with a broad red border. The yellow central portion contains red Turkish script, and the pole was surmounted with a gold sun finial[201].

OFFICERS

Traditionally, when the Tatar Khan raised an Army for war, the Tatar Bey: four Princes, who formed a Governing Council, and the Mursa: members of the four ruling families, each led their own contingents[202]. It is known that these Officers were representatives of the various aristocratic houses:

> "The Tatar have different degrees of rank. First is the Royal family, then those of Chirin, Mansoor, Sedjood, Arguin, and Baroon; and the ancient Mirzas form the high nobility, according to the above order."[203]

Accounts describing Tatar Officers from the 17th Century identify them as having, "the fanciest weapons and their insigne was a spear like those carried by pig-gelders"[204]. The use of a boar-spear as an Officer's insignia was also known to be used by Mameluke Officers. A 17th Century illustration of

---

193	Eton, 1798.
194	Eton, 1798.
195	Eton, 1798.
196	Eton, 1798.
197	Wittman, 1803.
198	Eton, 1798.
199	Williams, 2013.
200	McLean, 1818.
201	Suleyman, 1579.
202	Eton, 1798.
203	Dalvimart, 1802.
204	Williams, 2013.

the, "Khan of the Crimean Tatar[205], shows carrying an oxen-tail whip, with a red handle as a sign of his status. It was likely still used in the 18th Century. An illustration titled: Vezir Tatar Aghassi (Chef des Tatars Porteur de Lettres du Grand Vezir): Chief of Tatar carrying letters of the Grand Vizier[206]. This was a Senior Courtier in Tatar Government[207]. Dating from around the 1750s this shows a tall turquoise-blue fur covered wide-topped cylindrical peakless fez-styled hat with a green and yellow coil around the top. A long red loose open coat with long wide sleeves displays on the chest two large, patterned gold metal buttons, with chains (use to close the coat). The coat is worn over a white open collar, collarless shirt, and long orange skirt. A heavily gold embroidered green long coat, and fur shawl is visible under the coat. Light-blue Russian pants with lower leg gold embroidery, white socks and yellow Turkish slipper-shoes complete the dress.

TATAR DRESS

An 1802 illustration of a Tatar shows wide blue trousers and red boots[208]. A yellow Calpack: skin shaped hat with a deep black fur band around the brow is shown. An 1803 description of a Tatar hat: "Instead of a turban, they wear a yellow Calpack, round the inferior part of which is a broad band of black cloth."[209] The Calpack, was said to be specifically worn by Tatar Couriers carrying state correspondence for the Grand Vizier, who were stationed with the Army as Headquarters' Riders. An English Diplomat with the Turkish Army in Egypt, in 1800 observed Tatar wore turbans, and their heads were shaved[210]. The Diplomat remarked about the close similarity between Tatar Light Cavalry, and Lesghis: Cavalry from Georgia and Circassia (said to live at Mount Caucasus). These troops were identified by their unshaven heads, and wearing, "cap made of sheep's skin."[211]

An 1805 illustration of a Crimean Tatar Light Cavalry Soldier[212], is shown wearing a long buttoned green coat, with long close-fitting sleeves, and red collared shirt. Only yellow European riding boots, with distinctive high heels, are visible. A low flat-topped red conical hat with a brow band made of brown fur is depicted. The Soldier is armed with a long spear, and carries a Turkish bow, in its carry case. Extra arrows were carried in a separate quiver bucket slung over their back. A red ammunition box composed of three lines of musket cartridge tubes, on a thin red buckled waist strap is shown. While, an 1802 illustration depicts a waist ammunition bandolier belt with many individual musket cartridge tubes attached.

BATTLE TACTICS

Typically, two Tatar Light Cavalry Soldiers advanced toward their enemy, marking the best place for an attack, then followed by a larger force, of hundreds, and followed by thousands of Tatar Cavalry moving up, and delivering mass volleys of arrows at much greater distances, and greater accuracy than the defenders could respond with musket fire[213]. Traditionally, Tatar Cavalry employed swarming tactics:

205	Ralamb, 1658.
206	Sevket, 1907.
207	Eton, 1798.
208	Dalvimart, 1802.
209	Wittman, 1803.
210	Morier, 1801.
211	Morier, 1801.
212	Unknown, 1805.
213	Mugnai, 2014.

"[the Tatar] ... maneuvered rapidly, following the orders of the Khan's standard bearers who used visual signals to communicate and direct the mounted formations. The Tatar usually relied on flank attacks and surprise charges to break up the enemy's positions. When attacked by formed bodies of enemy Cavalry, the Tatar would frequently scatter and fake a retreat, shooting arrows from the saddle, then quickly re-group and attack the enemy whose formations were often strung out in pursuit. When confronted with impenetrable enemy formations, the Tatar poured arrow fire into the enemy's ranks, harried their detachments and cut off stragglers often wearing down the resistance of a stronger enemy."[214][215]

"The Tatar mode of fighting has no resemblance to European tactics; it is one continued scene of confusion and tumult ... Alternately flying and advancing in detached parties, many kinds of contest are carried on at once; the sabre the pike, and firearms, are all employed, and they fight alike on horseback or on foot, though the former is their most common mode."[216]

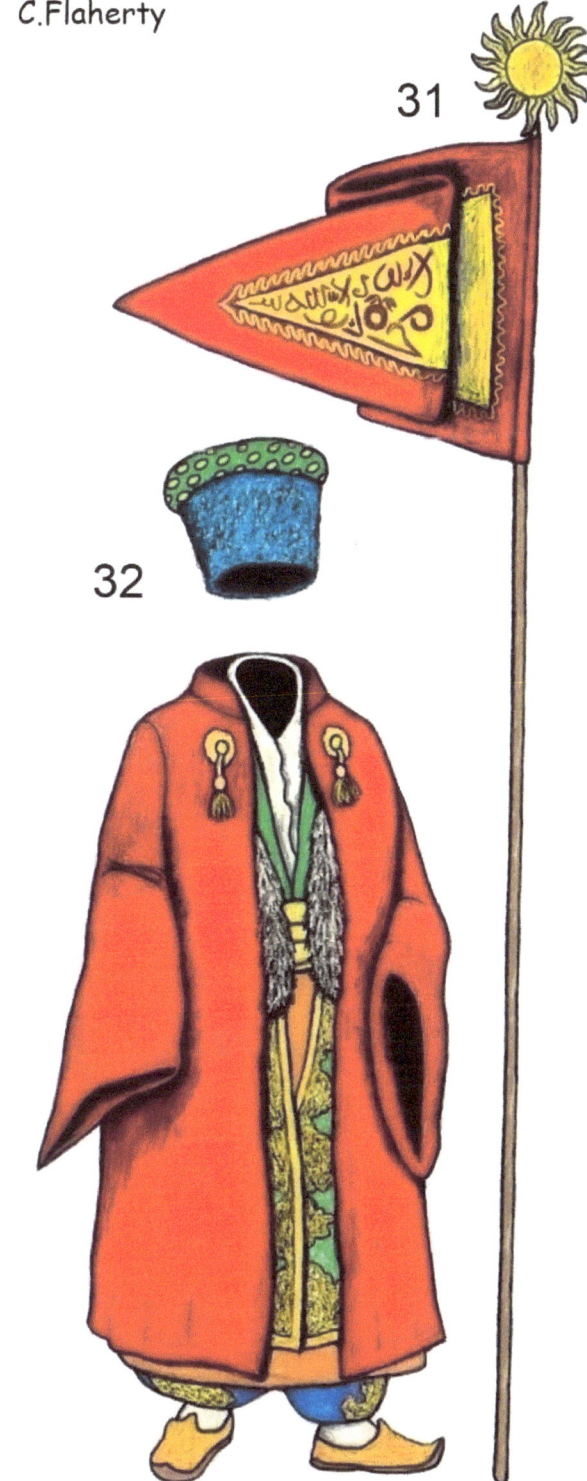

FIGURE 31: Tatar Advance Guard flag (16th Century).

FIGURE 32: Chief of Tatar (18th Century).

---

214   Eton, 1798.
215   Williams, 2013.
216   Eton, 1798.

FIGURE 33: Tatar Light Cavalry Soldier's ammunition belt (1802).

FIGURE 34: Tatar Light Cavalry Soldier's ammunition box (1805).

FIGURE 35: Tatar Light Cavalry Soldier (1805).

FIGURE 36: Tatar Couriers' hat Grand Vizier Headquarters' Riders (1803).

▼ Lithuanian Tatar of the Imperial Guard: Tartares Lituaniens de la Garde Imperiale Officer (1812). One squadron was attached to Konopka's 3rd Lancer Regiment of the Imperial Guard. Created at Vilna on 8 October 1812, raised from Muslim descendants of Genghis Khan who had settled in Lithuania during the Middle Ages.

CHAPTER 9: SIPAHI SORNAZEN

Sipahi Light Cavalry depicted in the 1810 Sultan Mahmud II Grand Review[217], shows a Sornazen: Trumpeter (also established under the New Order Army for use by Infantry, along with Tablzen: Drummers). The practice of using trumpet calls to lead Cavalry, and change formation may have been the result of European Cavalry training, as it is generally known that Sipahi were led by their Commander, and Sub-Commanders' flags. The Sipahi Sornazen is shown wearing a collarless knee-length light-blue coat, with tight-fitting long sleeves, red Russian pants, and red Turkish riding boots (like the two Officers), except the hat worn is a tall black conical fez. The Officers and the rest of the Soldiers wear red Cahouk: quilted top hats with a white Caouk: turbans. Another of the 1810 depictions show Sipahi Sornazen wearing red Cahouk with white Caouk, a collarless (open necked) knee-length blue coat, with tight-fitting long sleeves, and light-blue Russian pants and black Turkish riding boots.

Trumpets used by the Sipahi Sornazen appear in the 1810 Sultan Mahmud II Grand Review[218]. The instrument is long, and likely a Turkish Boru: brass trumpet or a bugle. This has small coloured pennants – red, white and white, hanging from its handle. Another illustration shows these as three or four white pennants only. The Boru was found in the Mehtar: Music Corps' Military Band. The Boru had an additional oval handle fitted, so the players' hand did not interfere with the instrument correctly vibrating (which could occur if they were directly holding it).

FIGURE 37: Sipahi Sornazen (1810).

FIGURE 38: Boru details (1810)

---

217   Unknown, 1810.
218   Unknown, 1810.

CHAPTER 10: TRADITIONAL CAVALRY ROLE IN BATTLE

The Cavalry role is known from mock-battles staged by the Turkish Army in 1596, in preparation for the Hungarian campaign as part of its training and drills[219]. Cavalry tactics remained unchanged into the 18th Century; and generally: "Turkish Cavalry never attack with combined strength, and in conformity with a regular plan"[220]. At the Battle of Kartal, in 1770 the Russians reported how the Turkish Army,

> "was arrayed in a crescent, with Anatolian Cavalry on the left flank, Rumelian … [Ottoman South-Eastern European] … Cavalry on the right, and the Tatar positioned in advance to operate as raiding parties. The Grand Vizier's huge, richly embroidered tent was pitched in the center … [the Janissary] … themselves at the heart of the camp"[221].

CAVALRY ATTACKS

Attacks by the Deli Cavalry was described in 1818: "The body of Light Cavalry … is very formidable in the charge; the attack is made in troops, and the rush on the enemy is accompanied with a shout of Allah! Allah! from every man, as an invocation to the deity. They boast of their temerity; and their conduct evinces a contempt for danger and fearlessness of death"[222]. Cavalry formed the main offensive wing of the Army and is known to have launched its attacks independently of the Foot Troops, and well ahead of the main fortified camp. It was also the case, that once the Cavalry attacked it left the battlefield. Known for somewhat erratic and uncontrollable behaviour, one possible explanation for this was the effect of opium use among the Cavalry. An English account from life in Turkey in the Napoleonic Era, commented that:

> "Smoking is a universal practice amongst the Turks; their tobacco is of the mildest and most fragrant kind … it seems indispensable to a military life, since throughout the Empire this propensity to smoking is equally indulged by the highest as well as the lowest ranks."[223]

Whereas smoking tobacco was common, it is generally known that opium consumption among Turkish, even by the 19th Century, "as a narcotic was limited"[224]. In 1800, an English Surgeon with the British Military Mission, sent to the Grand Vizier's Army, commented about general health among the Turkish Soldiers, remarked: "excesses in the use of smoking tobacco, and opium"[225]. Opium smoking in the Turkish camp is known, from an English account of the Egyptian Campaign, where he describes: "I went over … and got two whiffs of an opium pipe, which some of the Turks smoke until they are intoxicated."[226] Opium was produced in Anatolia, mostly for its medicinal properties[227]. A 17th Century account tells of opium laced meat used by animal-attendants to control

---

219 Mugnai, 2015.
220 Valentini, 1828.
221 Aksan, 2002.
222 McLean, 1818.
223 McLean, 1818.
224 Gingeras, 2014.
225 Wittman, 1803.
226 Low, 1911.
227 Kasaba, 1988.

▶ Illustrations show the Cavalry Soldier's pipe as large, and likely over four feet in length with brass end pieces.

C.Flaherty

lions in the Sultan's public processions[228]. An 18th Century English Traveler's account stated: "the use of opium, as is well known, is carried to excess in Constantinople."[229] Nevertheless, the same account suggested the problem of opium use was restricted to only some individuals, who were addicted, and known to be heavily intoxicated. A European commentary on the effect of opium use on Cavalry tactics: "It certainly does happen sometimes that an infuriated Turk, mounted upon a powerful horse, and perhaps intoxicated with opium, succeeds ... penetrating into the square"[230]. Another similar account, states:

> "Often the Turkish Cavaliers, half-drunk with opium, pierce even the most solid squares; and instances are not a wanting of their having, amidst the smoke and the strife, gone right through, and escaped on the opposite side without knowing where they had been."[231]

A Topracly Soldier is shown holding a long pipe[232][233][234]. Described as the, "indispensable articles with which a Turkish horseman never fails to provide himself, namely ... his pipe, which is fastened in front to the pommel of the saddle."[235]

DISMOUNTING

Turkish often trained Foot Soldiers to fight mounted. In the 17th Century, the 64th and 65th Cemaat Janissary Cavalry Orta: Battalion had existed. Long after disbandment, in 1623, there is a 1789 account that illustrates how Janissary were used as mounted Infantry: "[Janissary] ... having mounted behind the ... [Sipahi] ... leaped down, and fought by the side of their horse ... [after the battle] ... re-mounted their horses, took to flight."[236] European accounts from the 18th Century comment how the Turkish Soldier was trained as both a Foot Soldier, and Dragoon, "according to circumstances. If the ... [Sipahi] ... loses his horse, he immediately takes his place among the Infantry; and, in the same manner, the Janissary will mount, without hesitation, the first horse which chance throws in his way."[237] Sipahi were known to have directly supported Foot Soldiers in the battleline, from their flanking positions. It was also known that during defensive battles the Sipahi stationed themselves behind the Infantry, and could support them traditionally by firing their arrows, and by the 18th Century using their muskets. The Sipahi were also known to dismount fighting as Armoured Squads, or Dragoons using their muskets to give extra support. Strictly speaking, Turkish Infantry did not practice forming a square against Cavalry. The Janissary relied on the protection of the trench, or dedicated Cavalry, to protect the flanks and rear of their position. In the 18th Century, these Mounted Troops could be Janissary or Musketeers operating as Dragoons and fighting from their horses.

228	Mikhail, 2013.
229	Browne, 1799.
230	Valentini, 1828.
231	Alison, 1841.
232	McLean, 1818.
233	Sevket, 1907.
234	Dalvimart, 1802.
235	Wittman, 1803
236	Wright, 1799.
237	Valentini, 1828.

FORMATION TURNING, PURSUIT, BROKEN GROUND MANEUVER ENCIRCLING THE REAR, AND OUT-FLANKING SUPPORT

Sipahi deployed encircling the rear of Janissary Infantry and Artillery battleline, and readied to complete an encirclement of the enemy engaged at the entrenched or fortification barriers, sweeping-in from the flanks and behind them. The Sipahi role was to out-flank the attacking enemy; also feign retreats to encourage enemy frontal assaults onto a waiting Infantry and Artillery battleline. The key to their high-level maneuverability was that Turkish Cavalry never formally use Formation Wheeling, as each Cavalry Soldier would individually turn their own horse, rather than the whole unit performing a change of direction[238]. This allowed the Cavalry to turn in any number of directions:

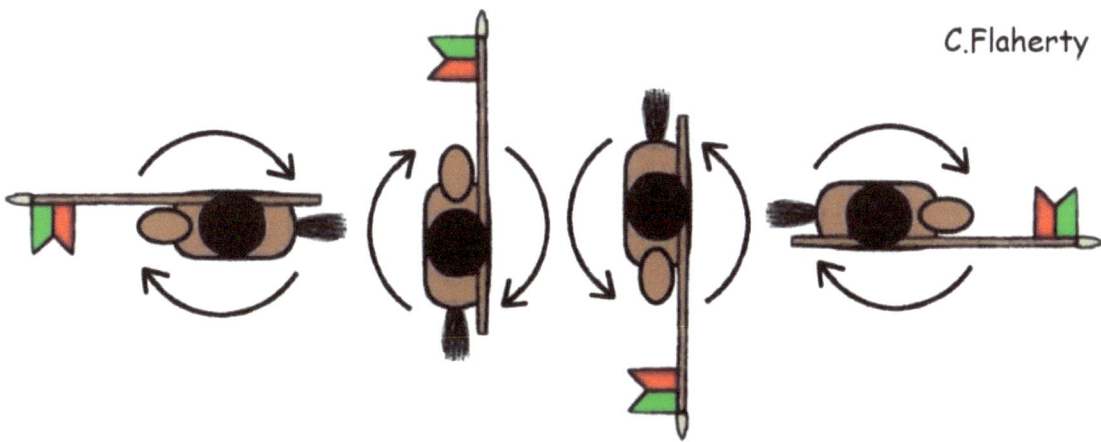

Sipahi specialized in pursuit attacks, the aim of which was to encircle the enemy's attack from behind, driving them from the rear onto the waiting Janissary and Artillery battleline. Turkish Cavalry, unlike their European counterparts trained for broken ground maneuver and attacks:

> "Accustomed from their infancy to climb the wooded declivities of their native hills, they early acquire an extraordinary skill and hardihood in horsemanship. A ... [Sipahi] ... will often ride at full gallop up and down hills, over torrents, through thick woods, along the edge of precipices, or where ... European ... [horse rider] ... would hardly venture even to walk. This extraordinary boldness increases when they act together in masses. When so assembled, they dash down rocks, and drive through brushwood in the most surprising manner. No obstacles intimidate, no difficulties deter, no disorder alarms them. The attacks of such bodies are in an especial manner to be dreaded in rugged or broken ground, where European Infantry deem it impossible for Cavalry to act at all. The heads of two or three horsemen are first seen peeping up through the brushwood, or emerging out of the steep ravines by which the declivities are furrowed, woe to the Battalion or Division that does not instantly stand to its arms, or form square on ... [the Turkish Cavalry] ... appearing. In an instant, five hundred or a thousand horsemen scale the rocks on all sides"[239].

---

238   Eton, 1798.
239   Alison, 1840.

A German account of broken ground attacks, states:

> "The Turkish Cavalry ... disperses itself in the mountains amid rocks and bushes, and then ... [emerge from a confined space] ... unawares by the most narrow paths, without fearing any disorder, since it is not accustomed to be in order. Hence it is extremely dangerous in an intersected country; it passes through places which seem impracticable, and suddenly appears upon the flank or rear of the enemy. Two or three men advance, and look about them: then you will see all at once five or six hundred"[240].

DOUBLE LINE FORMATIONS

Period illustrations of the Turkish Cavalry typically show them operating in long double line formations[241][242]. It is said that in battle the Sipahi, "do not engage en masse so much as the Janissary, but are more dispersed. It is however certain, that on these occasions each Troop or Squadron, whatever may be its strength, keeps together without mixing with the other troops."[243] Adopting rough order open lines, this allowed each Cavalry Soldier greater maneuverable space to change direction, and reorient their attack.

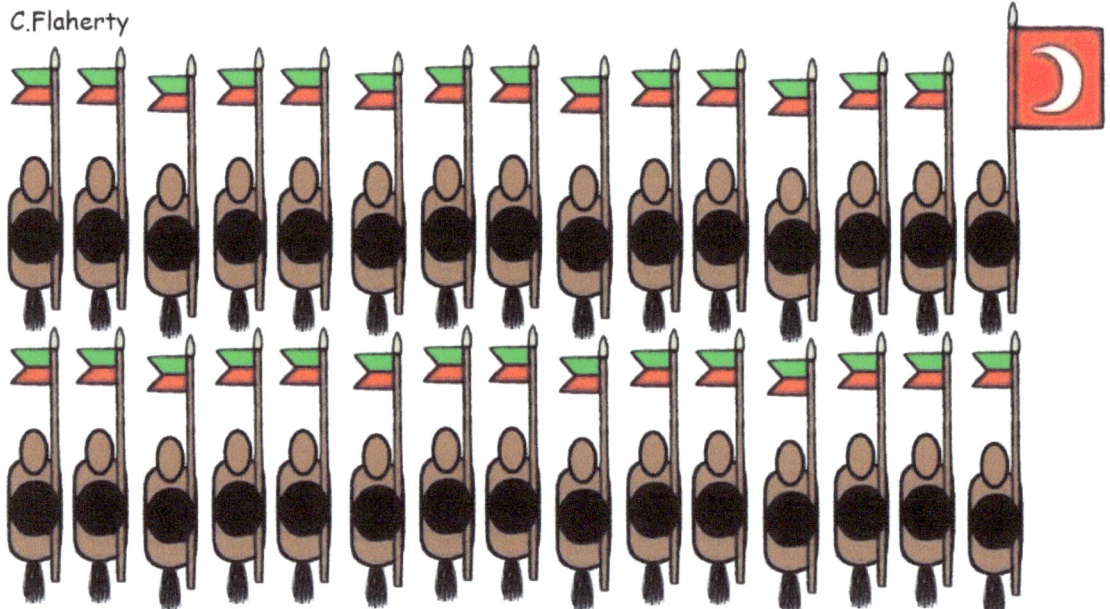

ATTACK DIVISION SEPARATION

It was likely, a Cavalry attack divided into three Divisions: Centre, Left and Right Wings, each under their own Subasis: Captains, which was basically a crescent-shaped deployment that allowed the Left- and Right-Wing Divisions to ride-ahead. Russian Infantry squares are reported being attacked on three sides at once by Turkish Cavalry.

240	Valentini, 1828.
241	Unknown, 1810.
242	Kobell, 1813.
243	Wittman, 1803.

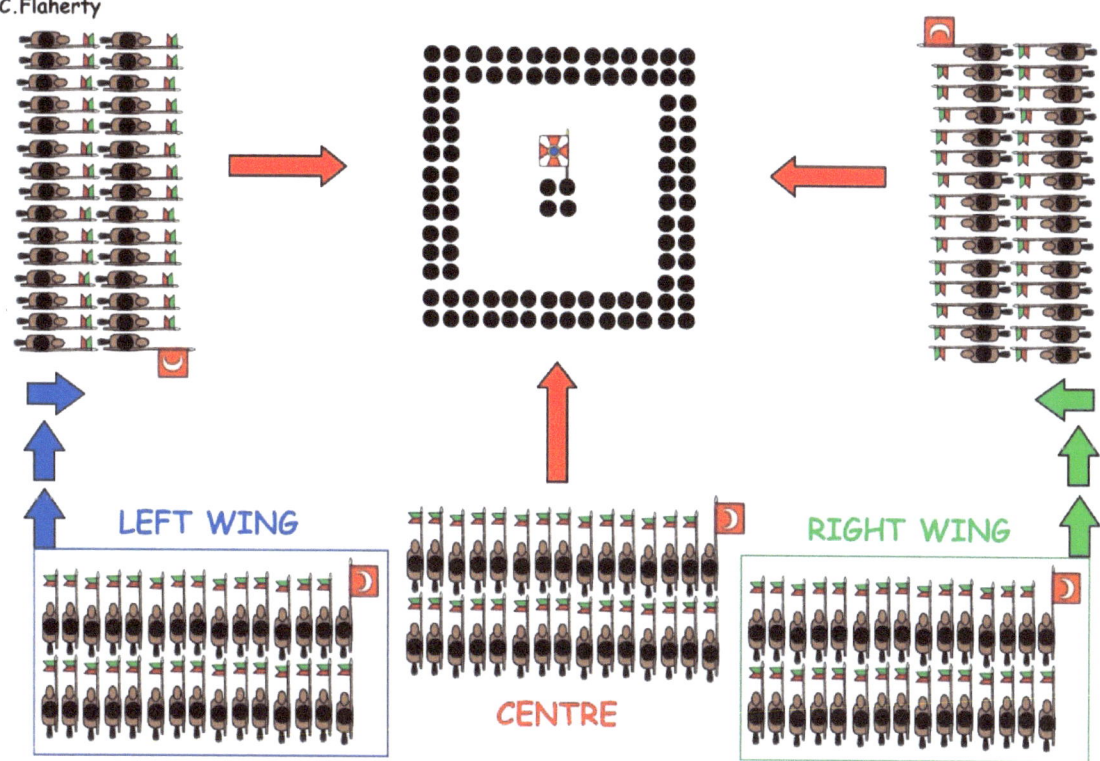

ATTACKS WITH SWORDS, JAVELIN, LONG SPEAR, OR LANCE

European 18th Century accounts tend to emphasize use of Kilij: curve-bladed scimitar-swords, as the main means of attack by Turkish Cavalry, as can be seen in this 1773 to 1774 Russian-Turkish War account: "just before day-break, he unexpectedly heard the cry of Allah! very near the spot where he was. He instantly arose, and perceiving a body of ... [Sipahi] ... coming towards him with uplifted sabres"[244]. This same form of attack was related in the late 18th Century Russian-Turkish Wars, "with loud cries they gallop forward upon their enemy; the Turkish ... [scimitar] ... is before their horses' heads, and in a few minutes a whole Regiment is cut to pieces."[245] It was said, that: "[Sipahi] ... wields ... [their scimitar] ... with a degree of perfection which we can scarcely hope to attain."[246] The acknowledged superiority of sword skills was seen, "founded partly on the quality of the weapon itself, and partly on their what may be termed national dexterity in handling it."[247] Turkish sword technique was different as well, from European styles:

> "The Turk, on the contrary, who gives rather a cut than a blow, makes it penetrate through helmet, cuirass etcetera and separates in a moment the head or the limbs from the body. Hence we seldom hear of slight wounds in an action of Cavalry with Turks."[248]

---

244 Anthing, 1813.
245 Alison, 1840.
246 Valentini, 1828.
247 Valentini, 1828.
248 Valentini, 1828.

The Turkish Kilij was known for its overall lightness, including its handle[249]. Because, of its curve, a downwards blow always had a cutting action, and its user was able, "[with] ... a small motion of the wrist ... [turn] ... the edge to the right or left"[250]. The skill at which Turkish used the sword, was largely due to, "every Soldier chooses his own sabre, and takes such a one as he can manage with ease"[251]. A German commentator from the period emphatically stated: "In pictures we see the ... [Sipahi] ... also armed with a short, pointed weapon, which, according to ancient descriptions of their mode of fighting, must have been a javelin. In my own experience, I never saw anything of the kind; and in no instance can this weapon be considered their principal arm"[252]. The German commentator later states:

> "In the campaign of 1811, individual Turks ... were often seen armed with a lance ... [taken from Cossacks] ... But this only tends to confirm my assertion that the lance or pike is but little used among the Turks, but that they became impressed with its advantages, and have made trials of it."[253]

However, another Napoleonic Era account, had this to say about the use of the lance: "Many of the ... [Turkish] ... Cavalry make use of the spear"[254]. A significant point to note about lance use, is that Turkish Cavalry Soldiers trained at an exercise, called the Djerrid: this consisted in riding at, "full speed after your antagonist, and lancing a stick (of about four feet long, and two-inches in circumference) at him; which he endeavors to parry with his own stick, or by stooping on his horse's neck."[255] This martial exercise would not have only given proficiency in the use of the lance, but also use of the sword. It can be assumed that a Turkish Cavalry Soldier was equally proficient at using, either or both weapons – the lance, or the sword. It was noted, due to the Djerrid training they, "lance the javelin with great force and dexterity."[256]

COMPARISON WITH EUROPEAN CAVALRY

The 18th Century general European military consensus was that Turkish Cavalry was superior to all other European Cavalry[257]. The relative weakness of European Cavalry, effected their tactics:

> "It cannot be denied that our Cavalry is inferior in comparison with the rest of our Army, when opposed to the Turks. Being completely dependent on the protection of the Batteries and squares of Battalions"[258].

> "[they are] ... no match in the shock of a charge for the superb steeds of the ... [Turkish] ... and the lance, even in the bravest hands, can hardly ward off the keen edge of the Damascus ... [scimitar]"[259].

A German commentary, notes in a period comparison that only Russian Cossack Cavalry were regarded as able to successfully counter the Turkish Cavalry[260].

---

249 Eton, 1798.
250 Eton, 1798.
251 Eton, 1798.
252 Valentini, 1828,
253 Valentini, 1828.
254 Eton, 1798.
255 Morier, 1801.
256 Wittman, 1803.
257 Eton, 1798.
258 Valentini, 1828.
259 Alison, 1840.
260 Valentini, 1828.

18th CENTURY TACTICS DEFEATING TURKISH CAVALRY

During the 18th Century Turkish warfighting continued largely unchanged, even though this was a period of rapid transformation in the weapons and tactics of European Armies, and a significant divergence in Western warfare had taken place, where parallel to development of conventional tactics of combined firepower and movement, developed an alternate, and highly specialized strategy for 'fighting the Turk'. Remarkably, from the European perspective, there developed effectively two different tactical systems: one to fight other European Armies, and one to fight Turkish Armies, that were in open contradiction of each other. Namely, the tactics used in the context of fighting Turkish, if used in a combat against other European Armies would have led to defeat. By the 18th Century, Turkish approach to the conduct of war in terms of its organization and military ethos was in stark contrast to European warfare, and reflected a unique set of circumstances. The overwhelmingly powerful massed Turkish Cavalry were better armed and displayed individually superior weapons handling skills, which surpassed that displayed by Austrian and Russian Cavalry[261]. A testament to the devastating effect of Turkish Cavalry sword mastery, was the well-known instance where Austrian Kurassier, were equipped with the lobster-tailed pot helmet as late as the 1780s, long after its use had died out elsewhere, introduced when campaigning against the Turkish[262]. These were not modern helmets for the period, the Austrians raided their State-Imperial Armoury for surviving 16th, and 17th Century helmets in the rush to equip their Cavalry to meet the threat posed by the Turkish Cavalry. In the case of the Russian Army of the late 18th Century the only Cavalry capable of meeting the Turkish on their own terms were the Cossacks[263]. Unable to cope with the Turkish Cavalry, Austrian and Russian Cavalry withdrew to shelter behind the Infantry and Artillery, in large marching squares. Adopting these dense slow-moving formations, if used against an opposing European Army of the period would have been a major tactical error, as opposing Artillery weapons and tactics had developed in this period to devastate such formations. The asymmetric response by Europeans, adopting tactics that were counter-intuitive to the prevailing orthodoxy allowed them to subject the massed attacks of the Turkish Cavalry, which in battles amounted to 20,000 or more Mounted Soldiers to the full-effect of massed musketry and Artillery fire – much the same way that the French Cavalry at Waterloo, in 1815 were destroyed in their massed and unsupported charges against Wellington's Infantry squares, and his Artillery; or where General Bonaparte used the Austrian-Russian method in Egypt, using Infantry and Artillery marching squares against the Mameluke, during the French Army march along the Nile River, at the Battle of Chebreiss, and at the Battle of the Pyramids (Embabeh), in 1798.

The adoption of the massed square by the Austrians, Russians and French exploited a critical flaw in Turkish Cavalry and Infantry organization; namely, its lack of effective leadership; and the piecemeal approach to conventional battle. The fatal flaw in Turkish campaigning practices was their inability to coordinate and concentrate their forces. The hallmark of the Turkish style of warfare was an initial attack by thousands of massed Cavalry, as the main offensive force on the battlefield. Regarded as the best in Europe, and feared with some justification for their sword mastery and valor in battle. Nevertheless, a charge unsupported by Infantry and mobile Artillery was destined for failure against the new tactics that had evolved in Austrian, Russian and later French Armies.

Turkish Cavalry often dispersed after their initial attack, riding away from the battlefield leaving the entrenched Infantry and Artillery in their fortified camps to await the final attack of the enemy Army. For individual Cavalry Soldiers, like their Janissary counterpart, fighting was largely based on an ethos of individual valor, and their tactics, and organization mirrored this approach. It was of-

---

261 Valentini, 1828.
262 Mollo, 1972.
263 Valentini, 1828.

ten commentated, in this period, that Turkish Soldiers fought as individuals rather than as organized Battalions[264].

Typically, like the Janissary, whole Alay: Regiment formations, would collect in rough-order groupings facing their opponents. Rough-order battle formations reflected the basic Janissary combat ethos: "every individual Turkish Soldier imagines himself opposed singly to the enemy's Army"[265]. The lack of control exercised by Officers, meant that individually Janissary made their own decision to fight or not: "he feels the impossibility of resisting it, and thinks it but reason able that he should retire."[266]

Turkish Cavalry Officers, like their Janissary counterparts, only had limited command authority, more akin to enforcing the laws that governed the life of Soldiers under their lead. In real terms, there was a Commander of a Regiment, that consisted of a thousand or more Soldiers, and several Junior Officers who led large bands. In the 18th Century, Officers carried a variety of large coloured flags to lead their Soldiers.

◀ Sipahi: Cavalry Officer.

264	Valentini, 1828.
265	Morier, 1801.
266	Morier, 1801.

CHAPTER 11: SULTAN'S HOUSEHOLD GUARD BANNERS, OFFICERS' COMMAND FLAGS AND LANCE PENNANTS

Numerous large square horizontally striped flags are pictured in the 1810 Sultan Mahmud II Grand Review[267]. The flags have triple pointed tails in various colour stripe combinations, consisting of three broad horizontal bars of purple, yellow and purple. Other variations include dark-green, yellow, dark-green bars; or purple, white and purple bars. The flag finial consists of a crescent mounted on a ball. Carried by various Sipahi, some of these are likely Cavalry Regiment flags; others, or possibly all these are various Officer's Command Flags:

> "[Turkish] … standards were larger than European standards. The first corps carried a yellow standard, the second a red one. The other Sipahi units carried red and white, white and yellow, green or white standards. The Sipahi also carried a tremendous mixture of smaller banners and flags into battle as well, with each Unit and Subdivision carrying its own banner, down to the troop level."[268]

A Napoleonic Era German commentator described other types of flags used by the Cavalry: "We often perceive pikes elevated among their troops, and bearing flags, upon which are represented the crescent, or a blood-red hand and a sabre: but these are not so much weapons as ensigns of war, under which the leaders of all ranks assemble their men, and conduct them to battle."[269] It is known, "[Sipahi] … do not, as the … [Janissary] … ascribe more honour to their kettle than their standard."[270] An 1801 account, also made this statement about the Sipahi flags, referring to the summoning of the Regiment, that they, "have their Officers … are obliged to assemble, properly armed and equipped, on the first summons, under the colours of their district … [Sanjakbeg: Governor]."[271][272] At the Battle of Heliopolis in Egypt, in 1800, when the Sipahi were making ready to charge, "the concentration of their standards along their whole line gave the French warning that it was approaching"[273]. An English account from Egypt, in 1800 provides a description of the use of Musketeer, or Orta: Battalion Officers' Command Flags, used in a similar fashion to the Cavalry attack: "The Turks formed … their Officers or Standard Bearers running to the front with the flags and holding them up, their front line formed upon them and discharged their muskets, then the flags started to the front again, and so on."[274]

LANCE PENNANTS

Most illustrations of late 18th Century Cavalry show only bare spears being used. It is known, "[a] … lance with either a red or yellow pennant … [is] … the traditional distinctive mark of a Sipahi."[275]

267	Unknown, 1810.
268	Johnson, 1988.
269	Valentini, 1828.
270	McLean, 1818.
271	Dalvimart, 1802.
272	Olivier, 1801.
273	Alison, 1842.
274	Low, 1911.
275	Johnson, 1988.

A large green lance pennant with a white crescent is seen in an 1817 illustration[276], that was particularly identified with the Dey of Algiers. An 1813 illustration of Sipahi shows full red lance pennants[277]. A larger lance pennant, for the same Sipahi, depicts a red pointed banner with a broad yellow border, displaying a yellow sun or crescent in the center, this is likely the Commander's or Regiment's flag.

SULTAN'S HOUSEHOLD GUARD CAVALRY DIVISION FLAGS

A 1732 illustration of a lance and its swallow-tailed pennant is described as used by the Capiculy: Cavalry[278]. The, "Capiculy or Soldiers of the Porte, or Capital … compose what may be strictly termed the Standing Army"[279]. This may be another description for the Sultan's Household Guard Cavalry. It is known that each of the Sultan's Household Guard Cavalry Divisions had their own distinctive flags[280]. A green banner was used by the Right-Garips Regiment[281][282]. The original illustration shows the flag displaying a cluster of three inward facing white crescents. This insignia is usually associated with the Pasha of Tripoli, in the early 1700s; as well it is described as one of the naval flags of the Sultan. The Left-Garips had a white banner[283]. A yellow banner was used by the Silahtar Regiment[284][285]. A version is known that displays double crescents[286]. Several 1732 illustrations depict flags leading troops that have this design[287]. A red banner was likely used by the Kapikulu Sipahi Regiment[288][289]. It also displayed a double crescent design[290][291]. The Left-Ulufecis Regiment used a red and yellow banner[292][293]. The Right-Ulufecis had a red and white banner.

An 1813 illustration show the Albanian Guard Cavalry using a red over green, with white crescent, lance pennant[294][295]. An illustration of an unidentified red over green pennant, without a white crescent is known[296]. It should be noted: "[the] … favorite colour for banners and standards among … [Turkish] … was red or green; or a mixture of the two colours."[297]

---

276 Unknown, 1817.
277 Kobell, 1813.
278 Marsigli, 1732.
279 Clarke, 1816.
280 Gush, 1975.
281 Sevket, 1907.
282 Gush, 1975.
283 Gush, 1975.
284 Sevket, 1907.
285 Gush, 1975.
286 Tyrrell, 1910.
287 Marsigli, 1732.
288 Sevket, 1907.
289 Gush, 1975.
290 Marsigli, 1732.
291 Tyrrell, 1910.
292 Sevket, 1907.
293 Gush, 1975.
294 Unknown, 1810.
295 Kobell, 1813.
296 Sevket, 1907.
297 Tyrrell, 1910.

FIGURE 39: Kapikulu Sipahi Regiment flag.

FIGURE 40: Left-Ulufecis Regiment flag.

FIGURE 41: Silahtar Regiment flag.

FIGURE 42: Right-Garips Regiment flag.

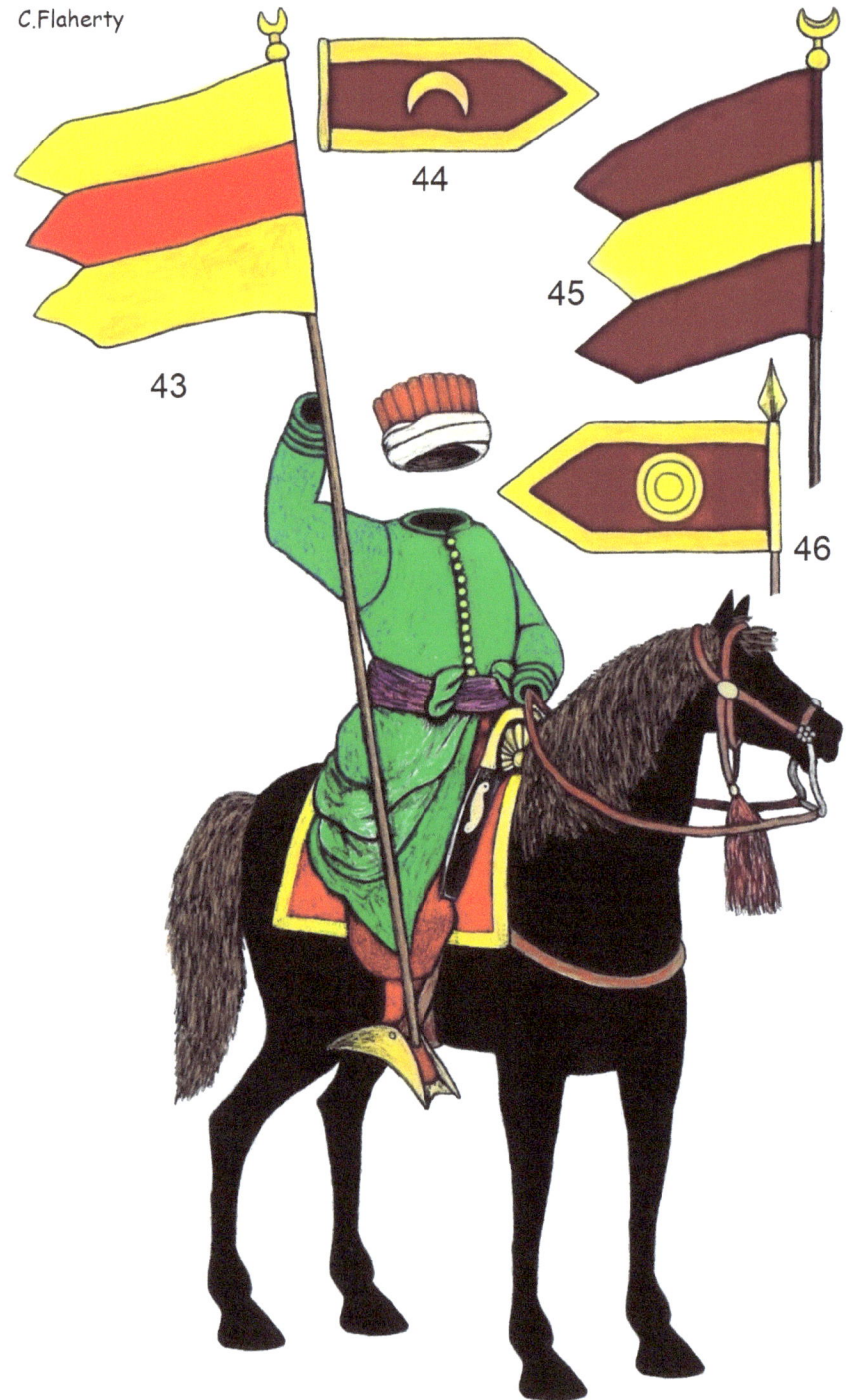

FIGURE 43: Sipahi Officer's Command flag.

FIGURE 44: Sipahi large lance pennant, likely Officer's Command or Regiment's flag (1813).

FIGURE 45: Sipahi Officer's Command flag.

FIGURE 46: Sipahi large lance pennant, likely Officer's Command or Regiment's flag (1813).

FIGURE 47: Sipahi Officer's Command flag.

FIGURE 48: Crescent finial detail.

FIGURE 49: Sipahi Officer's Command flag.

CHAPTER 12: WEAPONS, EQUIPMENT AND HORSE FURNITURE

Turkish Cavalry's weapons skills, in the 18th Century, were highly regarded: "every Turk is accustomed to the use of arms. They are all, perhaps, adepts in the use of the gun, the pistol, the ... [scimitar] ... and the lance. Being almost all ... hardy Cavaliers"[298].

KILIJ: CURVE-BLADED SCIMITAR-SWORD AND BROADSWORD VARIANT

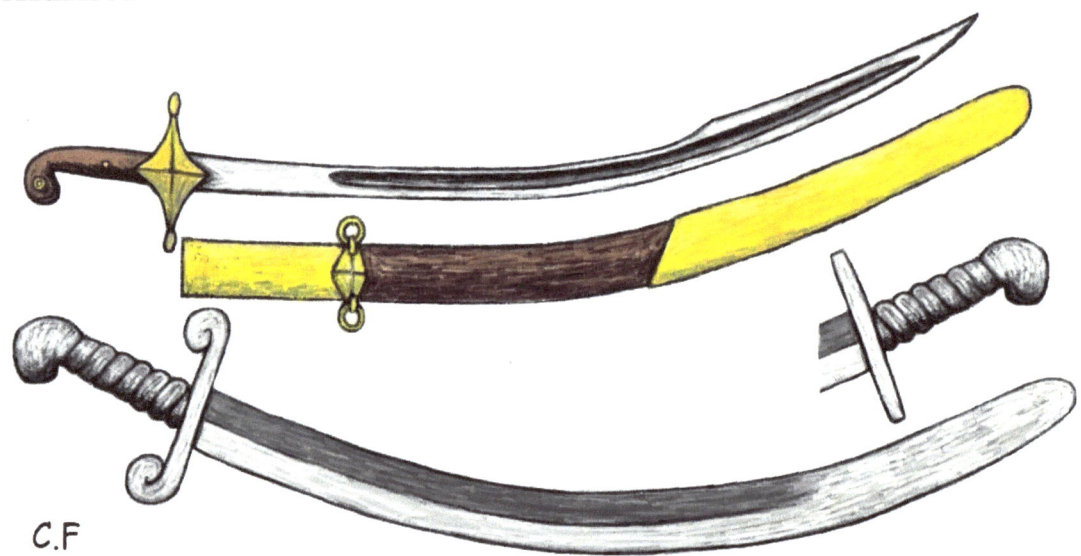

The most distinctive Turkish Cavalry weapon was the Kilij: curve-bladed scimitar-sword. Often called the, "Damascus scimitar"[299], these weapons after 1750 were rarely made from patterned-forged Wootz Steel, which had made these sword blades famous for their tough, shatter resistant and extremely sharp edges. By the late 18th Century, Kilij were shortened to a typical overall length of 27-inches, the blade itself formed into an acute curve. The first two-thirds of the blade was designed with a narrow width, while the last-third of its length (towards its point), called the Yalman: the blade flared, and was much wider. This feature was said to greatly add to the swords' cutting power. The back of the blade had a distinct 'T-shaped' cross section that allowed for greater blade stiffness without increasing its weight. The distinctive shape of the blade around its tip allows a thrust movement to be performed, in addition to the typical sabre sweep-action, or slicing cut. Kilij when compared to European sabres, it was said: "the edge of ... [European] ... sabres ... [were] ... never sharp enough, and the angle of the edge is too acute."[300] The Turkish weapon in comparison had a much thicker blade, with a broader edge. It is known, that the Kilij: "have one great defect, brittleness; they are apt to fly like glass by a blow given injudiciously, though a person used to cut with them will, without any danger of breaking ... or turning its edge, cut through an iron nail as thick as a man's finger."[301]

298	Alison, 1840.
299	Alison, 1840.
300	Eton, 1798.
301	Eton, 1798.

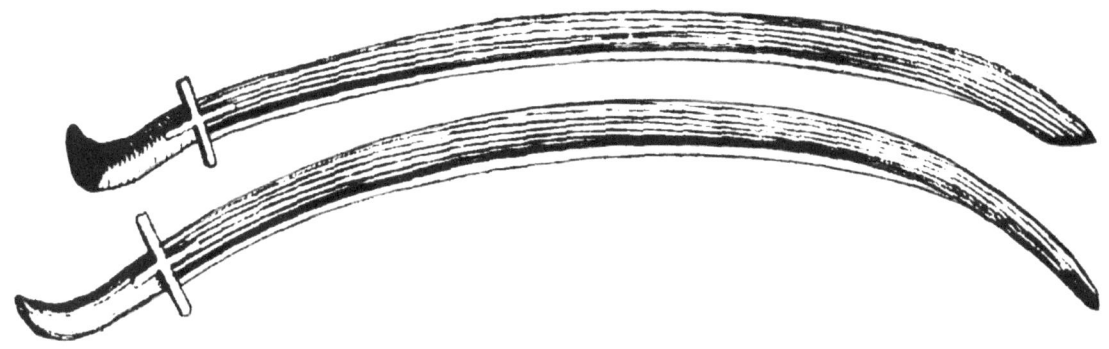

▲ A 1732 illustration of Turkish Kilij[302].

A Mameluke Zirkhli, and Light Cavalry Soldier armed with a Kilıj is known which appears to have a massive, curved flat blade without a T-shape, and without a fuller, that appears closer in proportions to a broadsword, and significantly, this weapon does not have a point, as the end is distinctly rounded. This feature is commonly seen on European executioners' swords designed for decapitation, the blade and the weapon being too large and heavy to effectively point, as only the blade edge can be used to strike. Only 1803 illustrations are known[303], and show a steel turned handle with the familiar scimitar pommel and either plain straight, or straight with end coils steel cross guards. It is interesting to note, illustrations show the swords slung in their scabbards with the blade uppermost[304], a technique used to preserve the blade-edge from wear to keep its sharpness. The wood scabbard was leather covered with brass fittings. Carry cords attached to the scabbard rings.

SHIELDS

A somewhat archaic large square shield slung over the back of a possibly Napoleonic Era Sultan's Household Soldier is known, that relates to the Albanian Guard Cavalry[305][306]. The 18th Century Cavalry iron-steel plate shield with a boss-spike covered the forearm[307][308], this is also shown as plain brown leather[309], or leather with a broad metal rim[310]. The shield was usually, "strapped to the left arm ... this would be round and up to 30-inches in diameter"[311]. It was used to protect the rein-hand from sword strikes. Shields were heavy enough to protect even against musket fire at extended ranges. Traditionally, in the 15th and 16th Centuries, Turkish used the Kalkan: round wickerwork shield made from spirally plaited cane, that was stitched with fabric around a central hand holding boss, made of wood[312]. By the 17th and 18th Centuries, these were reinforced with an iron boss, rim, and connecting iron strips radiating towards the centre. Kalkan could also be reinforced with iron or brass over-lapping plates.

302	Marsigli, 1732.
303	Walsh, 1803.
304	Sevket, 1907.
305	Unknown, 1810.
306	McLean, 1818.
307	Sevket, 1907.
308	Gush, 1975.
309	Unknown, 1805.
310	Walsh, 1803.
311	Gush, 1975.
312	Gush, 1975.

JAVELIN, LONG SPEAR, OR LANCE

A 1732 set of illustrations show various Cavalry lance, spear and javelin head types used[313]. These are a variety of small pointed, or large leaf or triangular blades, or have a line of weights following the blade-head. The blade was secured to the shaft with a tang and pegs, or by a long-riveted socket-tube. Late 18th Century Cavalry Soldiers depicted with spears or lances[314][315], show the weapon had a long triangular head, and metal spear-butt on the end of a long natural wood pole that looks to be about nine feet in length; however, twelve to fourteen feet in length are also described[316]. Spear weapons used varied greatly:

> "Frequently ... horsemen carry pikes and javelins of different lengths, of which the shorter ones are ... secured to the saddle. Some of these weapons are six feet or more in length, with an iron point ... nearly a foot long, to the bottom of which is attached a tassel made of feathers, or hair."[317]

> "Many ... have the privilege of selecting their own weapons; they carry pikes of different lengths, usually about six feet, having an iron point or spear, sometimes ornamented with a tassel, composed of feathers or hair."[318]

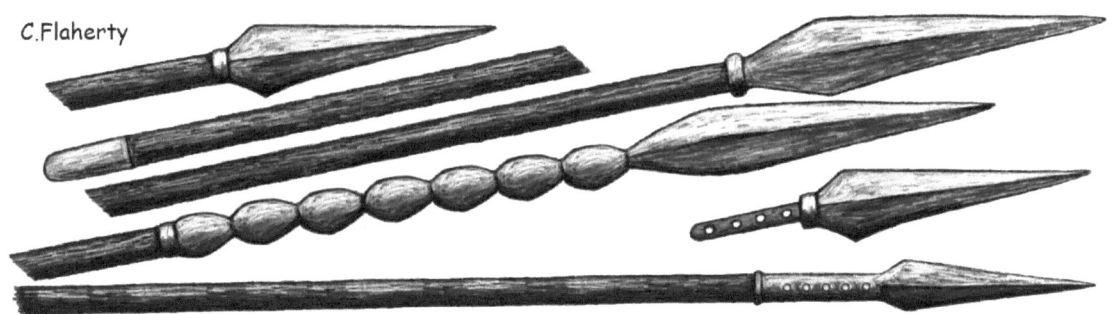

C.Flaherty

TURKISH BOW USE

Traditionally, Janissary used Turkish bow as their main weapon. The bow was a recurved composite, or classic Asiatic type. It had a maple wooden core, animal horn covered the belly-underside (the side facing the archer), and sinew lined its front side, with the layers secured with animal glue. The curvature of the Turkish bow is generally more extreme, than most composite, or classic Asiatic types, as when the bow is unstrung its Kasan: arms curl forward into a 'C-shape' (and in some cases the ends touch). The grip area is not recessed like other Asiatic bows, as it is flat on the inward side, while the front of the grip bulges outwards. The Turkish bow was classically known to be difficult to string, requiring a force of 99-pounds to pull. The immensely powerful bow could shoot an arrow well past musket range. An arrow was shot 434 meters, at a 1910 archery contest at Le Touquet, France, using an old Turkish bow.

The brown leather bow case, like the separate quiver-bucket (on a shoulder strap) appears to have been universal type, as the same versions are shown used by Cavalry Soldier from Bagdad[319]; Deli

---

313 Marsigli, 1732.
314 Unknown, 1810.
315 Kobell, 1813.
316 Wittman, 1803.
317 Wittman, 1803.
318 McLean, 1818.
319 Unknown, 1805.

▶ A 1732 illustration of a Turkish bow, and case[320].

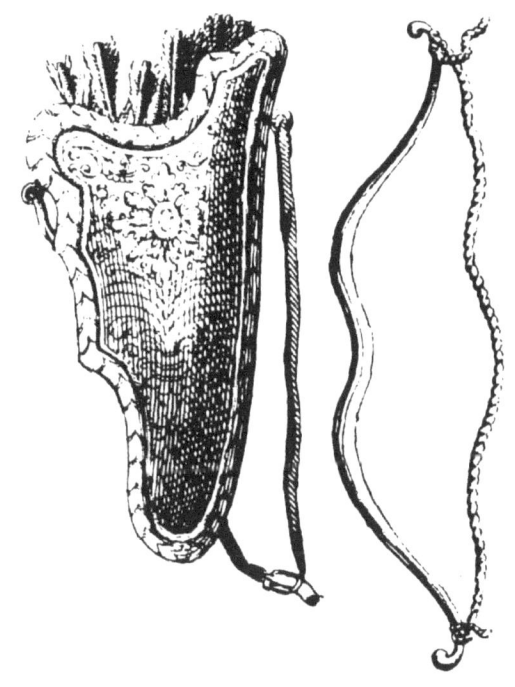

Cavalry Soldier from the Aleppo Vilayet: Province Governorship[321]; and Tatar[322], all around 1805. The bow case is shaped for the lower half of the bow, and either some large Islamic script, or floral work covering the outer side. It had side straps to hang from the waist sash or over the shoulder.

CARTRIDGE BOX

During the 1770s Russian-Turkish War, it was noted, that due to rain which soaked Turkish uniforms, "as they used small pockets, instead of cartridge-boxes, their powder was moistened, and rendered unfit for use."[323] An 1803 dated illustration shows a small ammunition box hanging at the back of several Turkish Soldiers, which may have also been used by Cavalry, directly under the waist sash[324]. A large black European-styled cartridge box is depicted slung over the back of a possible Cavalry Soldier in the 1810 Sultan Mahmud II Grand Review[325], with a white adjustable (as three buckle loops are shown) shoulder carry strap.

SADDLES AND SCHABRACKE

A surviving example of a Cossack brown with red and yellow decorations padded leather saddle was known used in the 18th Century by Janissary[326]. This may not have needed a Schabracke to protect the horse's back. A brown saddle with a lower chair back, and white square Schabracke is depicted used by a Deli Cavalry Soldier from around 1803[327]. An 1805 illustration of a Deli Cavalry Soldier from Aleppo[328], shows a brown padded Cossack leather type of saddle with square light-blue Schabracke with a double yellow line-edging. Sipahi saddles shown in the 1810 Sultan Mahmud II Grand Review[329], show a black high-fronted and highchair saddle with brass decorations, along with small square Schabracke in various colours: blue, red, purple with white or yellow tape edges, which do not appear to match the colours worn by the Sipahi themselves.

320	Marsigli, 1732.
321	Unknown, 1805.
322	Unknown, 1805.
323	Anthing, 1813.
324	Wittman, 1803.
325	Unknown, 1810.
326	Askeri Muze.
327	Phillips, 1803.
328	Unknown, 1805.
329	Unknown, 1810.

FOOTWEAR, SPURS AND POINTED STIRRUPS

Cavalry, in particular the Deli traditionally wore, "yellow boots"[330]. A Napoleonic Era illustration shows a Deli wearing red boots[331][332]. Most Cavalry wore Turkish riding boots, that were short soft calf boots and tight fitting. However, 1805 dated illustration of a Cavalleristen von Bagdad: Cavalry Soldier from Bagdad[333], shows wearing yellow European riding boots, with distinctive high heels; as does an 1805 dated illustration of a Deli Cavalry Soldier from the Aleppo Vilayet: Province Governorship[334]; and a Tatar[335]. It is known, "spurs are very seldom included in 16th Century Persian or Turkish miniatures."[336] Pointed stirrups, and the boot heal were used to guide the horse: "The Turkish saddle is somewhat inconvenient to Europeans; and as spurs are not employed, the rider is obliged to have recourse to his stirrups when he wishes the animal on which he is mounted to quicken his pace."[337] Mounted Soldiers depicted wearing yellow European riding boots, with distinctive high heels, are also shown using conventional stirrups. It is known Renaissance Era Deli Cavalry used, "foot-long spurs"[338]. Use of these long spurs may be unusual. However, it is said that the Deli, "rode short fatty horses and they therefore needed these long spurs"[339]. These animals may have been breeds of horse similar to Icelandic and Fjord who are squat, fatter and with thick hair coats.

WATER BOTTLES

Turkish Cavalry carried, "a leathern bottle, or perhaps several, filled with water, and reaching from the saddle to beneath the belly of the horse"[340].

---

330   Gush, 1975.
331   Phillips, 1803.
332   Wittman, 1803.
333   Unknown, 1805.
334   Unknown, 1805.
335   Unknown, 1805.
336   Titley, 1983.
337   Wittman, 1803.
338   Gush, 1975.
339   Mallet, 1684.
340   Wittman, 1803.

C.Flaherty

FIGURE 50: Deli Cavalry Soldier from Aleppo saddle (1805).

FIGURE 51: Deli Cavalry Soldier's saddle (1803).

FIGURE 52: Janissary (Cossack padded leather) saddle (18th Century).

FIGURE 53: Sipahi saddle (1810).

BIBLIOGRAPHY

Agoston, G. 2011 Military Transformation in the Ottoman Empire and Russia, 1500–1800. Kritika: Explorations in Russian and Eurasian History. Volume 12. Issue 2.

Aksan, V.H. 2007 Ottoman Wars 1700-1870: An Empire Besieged. Routledge.

Aksan, V. 2002 Breaking the Spell of the Baron de Tott: Reframing the Question of Military Reform in the Ottoman Empire, 1760-1830. The International History Review. XX. Volume 2 (June).

Alison, A. 1842 History of Europe from the Commencement of the French Revolution in 1789, to the Restoration of the Bourbons in 1815. Volume 2. New York: Harper & Brothers.

Alison, A. 1841 History of Europe from the Commencement of the French Revolution in 1789 to the Restoration of the Bourbons in 1815. Volume 7. Baudry, Paris.

Alison, A. 1840 History of Europe from the Commencement of the French Revolution in 1789 to the Restoration of the Bourbons in 1815. Volume 8. Blackwood.

Anthing, J.F. [Translator] 1813 History of the Campaigns of Count Alexander Suworow-Rymnikski. London: W. Green and T. Chaplin. 1 Crane-Court, Fleet-Street.

Askeri Muze [Militarmuseum]. Janissary Saddle. Istanbul.

Badisches Landesmuseum. Turkish Tug from the Late 17th Century. Karlsruhe.

Bowles, C. 1801 Bowles's Universal Display of the Naval Flags of all Nations in the World. London: Carington Bowles.

Brindesi, J. Bour, C. (Lithographer) 1850 Choubara Neferi, Soldat of the 1st Reform of Sultan Mahmoud II. Illustration. Vinkhuijzen, H.J. [Collection]. New York Public Library [The]. Image ID: 416350.

Browne, W.G. 1799 Travels in Africa, Egypt, and Syria, from the Year 1792 to 1798. London: T. Cadell (Junior), and W. Davies, Strand.

Brouillet, J. 1961 Les Uniformes de la Campagne d'Egypte [The Uniforms of the Campaign of Egypt] 1798-1801. Orleans. Loose-Leaf Series of 90 Pages, with Two Card Illustrations Each: From Various Illustrators (Collected into Series): Jacques Brouillet Presente: La Collaboration d'un Groupe d'Amis Artistes et Collectionneurs: Serie de 90 Planches, de 2 Cartes Chacune: Sur les Lenues Partees Durant Cotte Campagne par les Differentes Armees Belligerantes.

Buyukakca, M.C. 2007 Ottoman Army in the Eighteenth Century: War and Military Reform in the Eastern European Context. Graduate Thesis. Middle East Technical University.

Castellan, A-L. 1812 Mamlouks. Illustrations de Histoire des Othomans. Moeurs, Usages, Costumes des Othomans, et Abrege de Leur Histoire. Paris: Nepveu.

Chalcondyles, L. [Artus, T. Translator] 1662 Historie des Turcs. Volume II. Paris.

Clarke, H. 1816 The History of the War: From the Commencement of the French Revolution to the Present Time. Volume 1. T. Kinnersley.

Creasy, E.S. 1878 History of the Ottoman Turks: from the Beginning of their Empire to the Present Time. London: R. Bentley.

Dalvimart, O. Miller, W. 1802 The Costume of Turkey: Illustrated by a Series of Engravings; with Descriptions in English and French. London: T. Bensley.

Douwes, D. 2000 Ottomans in Syria: A History of Justice and Oppression. I.B.Tauris.

Dunn, J.P. 2013 Khedive Ismail's Army. Taylor & Francis Ltd.

Eric, G. Matson, E. 1914 Early 20th Century Photograph of an Arab Bedoin Warrior. Library of Congress. Photograph Collection. LC-DIG-matpc-06823.

Eton, W. 1798 A Survey of the Turkish Empire. London: T. Cadell and W. Davies, Strand.

Gingeras, R. 2014 Heroin, Organized Crime, and the Making of Modern Turkey. OUP Oxford.

Grant, C. 2007 Napoleon's Campaign in Egypt. Volume 2: The British Army and Allies. Partizan Press.

Goffman, D. 2002 The Ottoman Empire and Early Modern Europe. University Press, Cambridge.

Goodwin, J. 1998 Lords of the Horizons: A history of the Ottoman Empire. Picador.

Gush, G. 1975 Renaissance Armies: 1480–1650. PSL, UK.

Hammer-Purgstall, J. [Freiherr Von]. 1837 Histoire de L'Empire Ottoman. J.J. Hellert: Paris.

Herold, J.C. 1962 Bonaparte in Egypt. New York: Harper & Row.

Haythornthwaite, P.J. Warner, C. 1998 Uniforms of the French Revolutionary Wars 1789-1802. Sterling Publishing Company Incorporated.

Johnson, W.E. Bell, C. 1988 The Ottoman Empire and the Napoleonic Wars. Partizan Press.

Kasaba, R. 1988 The Ottoman Empire and the World Economy: The Nineteenth Century. Suny Press.

Kapidagli, K. 1803 Sultan Selim III in Audience. Painting. Topkapi [Palace Museum].

Knotel, H. 1963 [-1950] Guide Indigene en Egypt, 1799. Illustration.

Kobell, W.A.W. 1813 [-1809] Turkish Cavalry. Artaria & Company: Vienna.

Kobell, W.A.W. 1813 [-1809] Turkish Infantry. Artaria & Company: Vienna.

Kolcak, O. 2012 The 17th Century Military Development and the Ottomans: The Ottoman-Habsburg Wars of 1660-64. Dissertation.

Kunsthistorische Museum. Turkish Tug. Vienna.

Laking, G.F.L 1964 Persian Helmet Modelled with a Face, and Horns. Wallace Collection Catalogues: Oriental Arms and Armour. London: The Trustees of the Wallace Collection.

London Illustrated News. 1882 Khedive's Zirkhagi: Iron Men (Cuirassiers). Number 2218. Volume XXXI (3 June).

Low, E.B. MacBride, M. [Edited & Introduction] 1911 With Napoleon at Waterloo. London: Francis Griffiths.

MacFarlane, C. 1829 Constantinople in 1828. London: Saunders and Otley, Conduit Street.

McLean, T. [John Heaviside Clark] 1818 The Military Costume of Turkey. London: Thomas McLean.

McNabb, J.B. 2017 A Military History of the Modern Middle East. ABC-CLIO.

Mallet, A.M. 1684 Les Travaux de Mars, ou L'Art de la Guerre. Paris.

Marsigli, L.F. 1732 L'Etat Militaire de l'Empire Ottoman. Amsterdam.

Mikhail, A. 2013 The Animal in Ottoman Egypt. Oxford University Press.

Mollo, J. 1972 Military Fashion: A Comparative History of the Uniforms of the Great Armies from the 17th Century to the First World War. Barrie and Jenkins.

Morier, J.P. 1801 Memoir of a Campaign with the Ottoman Army in Egypt, from February to July 1800. London: J. Debrett.

Mugnai, B. Flaherty, C. 2014 Der Lange Turkenkrieg (1953-1606). Volume 1: The Long Turkish War - Habsburgs Arrest the Ottoman Advance. Soldiers & Weapons 024. Soldiershop.

Mugnai, B. Flaherty, C. 2015 Der Lange Turkenkrieg (1593-1606) Volume 2: The Long Turkish War. Soldiers & Weapons 027. Soldiershop.

Musee de l'Armee [The]. 1798 Harnachement De Mamelouk. No. Inventaire: 5171I, Cd 73.

Musee de l'Armee [The]. 1798 Toug Ottoman. No. Inventaire: Aa 8.

Nicolle, D. 1998 Armies of the Ottoman Empire 1775-1820. Osprey Publishing.

Nicolle, D. 1995 The Janissaries. Osprey Publishing.

Ocak, D. 2016. Gift and Purpose: Diplomatic Gift Exchange Between the Ottomans and Transylvania During the Reign of Istvan Bathory (1571-1576). MA Thesis, Central European University, Budapest.

Olivier, G.A. 1801 Travels in the Ottoman Empire, Egypt, and Persia, Undertaken by Order of the Government of France, During the First Six Years of the Republic. Volumes 1-2. London: T.N. Longman, O. Rees, Paternoster- Row, T. Cadell (Jun.), and W. Davies.

Ozturk, T. 2016 Egyptian Soldiers in Ottoman Campaigns from the Sixteenth to the Eighteenth Centuries. War in History. Volume 23. Issue 1.

Pitt Rivers Museum. The Beautiful Warrior: Early 19th Century Persian Helmet Depicting the Face of a Pre-Islamic Demon or Div.

Phillips, R. 1803 Delhi-Turkish Light Cavalry. Illustration. Anne S.K. Brown Military Collection. BDR: 233466.

Phillips, R. [Editor] 1803 The Monthly Magazine, or, British Register. Volume 16. Part 2. London: J. Adland.

Ralamb, C. 1658 [-1657] Tatar. Ralamb Costume Book. Royal Library in Stockholm.

Ralamb, C. 1658 [-1657] Khan of the Crimean Tatar. Ralamb Costume Book. Royal Library in Stockholm.

Rigo, J. Lebref (et Cie). 1840 Kabyle: A Berber of Algeria or Tunisia. Illustration. Vinkhuijzen, H.J. [Collection]. New York Public Library [The]. Image ID: 826678.

Robinson, H.R. 1967 Oriental Armour. New York: Walker and Company.

Roubicek, M. 1978 Modern Ottoman Troops, 1797-1915: In Contemporary Pictures. Franciscan Printing Press.

Scott, W. 1827 The Life of Napoleon Bonaparte. Volume VI. Paris: A. and W. Galignani.

Sevket, M. [Mahmoud Chevket Pasha] 1907 L'Organization et les Uniformes de l'Armee Ottomanne. Premiere Partie.

Shaw, S.J. 1965 The Nizam-i Cedid Army Under Sultan Selim III 1789-1807. Oriens. Volumes 18/19 (1965/1966).

Strathern, P. 2008 Napoleon in Egypt. Random House.

Suleyman. 1579 Miniature [Painting]: Tatar as Avantgarde on the Szigetvar Campaign, 1566. History of Sultan Suleyman [Tarih-i Sultan Suleyman (Zafarnama)]. Dublin: Chester Beatty Library, MS 413, fol. 82a.

Titley, N.M. 1983 Early Ottoman Miniature Painting: Two Recently Acquired Manuscripts in the British Library. British Library Journal.

Turnbull, S. 2003 The Ottoman Empire 1326-1699. Osprey Publishing.

Tyrrell, F. H. 1910 Old Turkish Military Costumes and Standards. The Imperial and Asiatic, Quarterly Review and Oriental and Colonial Record. Third Series. Volume XXX. Numbers 59 & 60 (July-October).

Unknown. 1600 [-1805] Turkische Cavallerie (Hand Dated 1795). Illustration. Vinkhuijzen, H.J. [Collection]. New York Public Library [The]. Image ID: 416250.

Unknown. 1799 History of the Life and Campaigns of Count Alexander Suworow Rymnikski. J. Legg.

Unknown. 1800 Soldat Egyptien. Illustration. Anne S.K. Brown Military Collection. BDR: 233470.

Unknown. 1805 Aga General der Reuterey: General of the Cavalry (Hand Dated 1805). Illustration. Vinkhuijzen, H.J. [Collection]. New York Public Library [The]. Image ID: 416271.

Unknown. 1805 Cavalleristen von Bagdad (Hand Dated 1805). Illustration. Vinkhuijzen, H.J. [Collection]. New York Public Library [The]. Image ID: 416273.

Unknown. 1805 Cavalleristen von Haleb, Deli Genannt (Hand Dated 1805). Illustration. Vinkhuijzen, H.J. [Collection]. New York Public Library [The]. Image ID: 416272.

Unknown. 1805 Crimean Tatar (Hand Dated 1805). Illustration. Vinkhuijzen, H.J. [Collection]. New York Public Library [The]. Image ID: 416274.

Unknown. 1810 Turkish Cavalry Soldier Featuring Trumpeters (Hand Dated 1810). Illustration. Vinkhuijzen, H.J. [Collection]. New York Public Library [The]. Image ID:416283.

Unknown. 1810 [-1817] Turkish Officer of the Sipahi. Illustration. Vinkhuijzen, H.J. [Collection]. New York Public Library [The]. Image ID: 416308.

Unknown. 1810 [-1817] Mahmud II Grand Review. Illustration. Vinkhuijzen, H.J. [Collection]. New York Public Library [The]. Image ID: 416284; 416285; 416288; 416289.

Unknown. 1817 Turkish Cavalry Soldier (Hand Dated 1817). Illustration. Vinkhuijzen, H.J. [Collection]. New York Public Library [The]. Image ID: 416293.

Unknown. 1820 Egyptian Zirkhagi Cavalry Soldier. Illustration. Vinkhuijzen, H.J. [Collection]. New York Public Library [The]. Image ID: 1606998.

Uyar, M. Erickson. E.J. 2009 A Military History of the Ottomans: From Osman to Ataturk. ABCCLIO.

Valentini, G.W. [Anonymous Translator] 1828 Military Reflections on Turkey. C. & J. Rivington: London.

Valfrio. 1856 Arab Sentry of the Turkish Irregular Army. London Illustrated News (12 January).

Vorstellung Uber der Kriegswesen. 1800 Turkish Military Insignia, Standards and Regalia, Circa 1600. Book Illustration. Anne S.K. Brown Military Collection. BDR: 233575.

Walsh, T. 1803 Journal of the Late Campaign in Egypt. Cadell & Davies, Strand, London.

Williams, B.G. 2013 The Sultan's Raiders: The Military Role of the Crimean Tatars in the Ottoman Empire. The Jamestown Foundation, May.

Wittman, W. 1803 Travels in Turkey, Asia-Minor, Syria, and Across the Desert into Egypt During the Years 1799, 1800, and 1801, in Company with the Turkish Army, and the British Military Mission. London: Richard Phillips.

Wright, J. 1799 History of the Life and Campaigns of Count Alexander Suworow Rymnikski. Publisher: J. Wright, London.

OTHER TITLES BY THE SAME AUTHOR

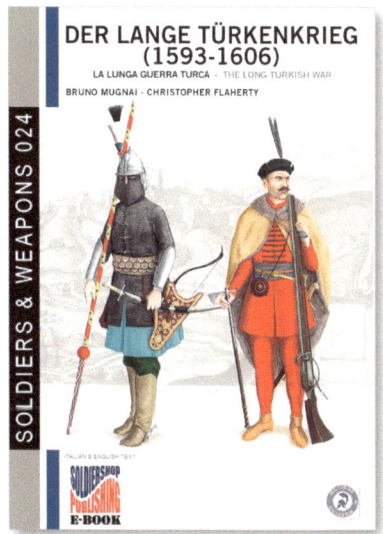
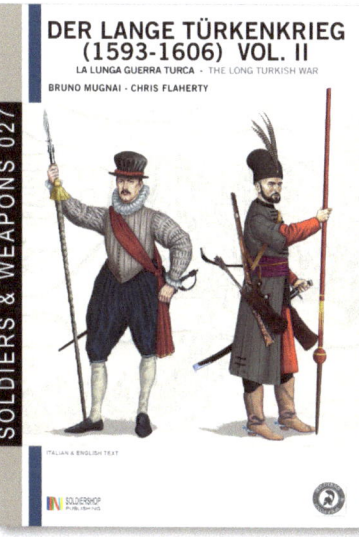
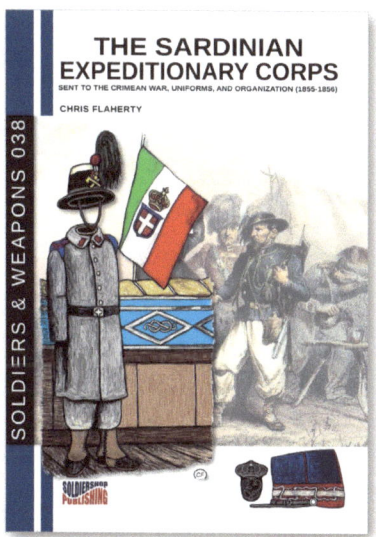
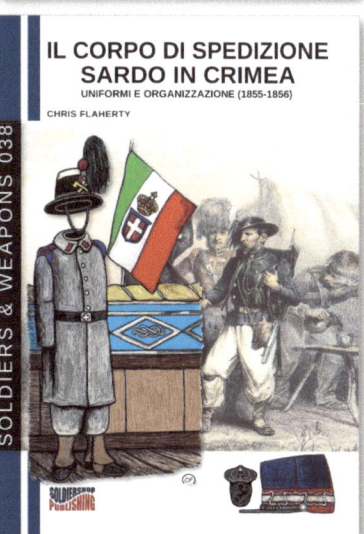
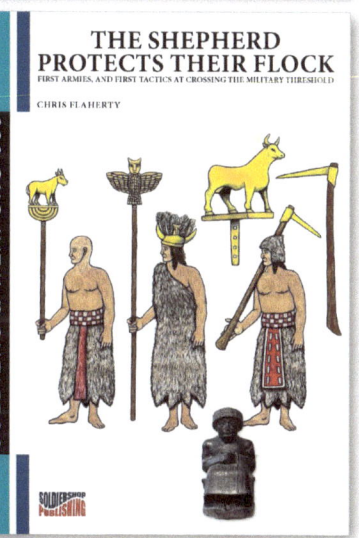
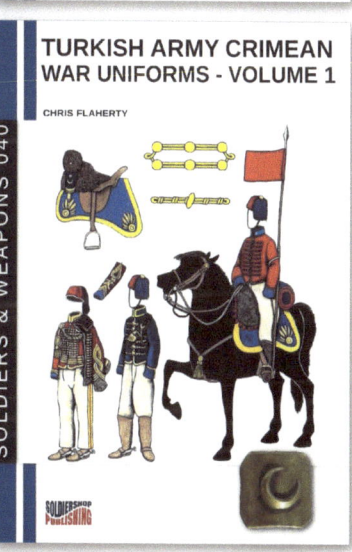
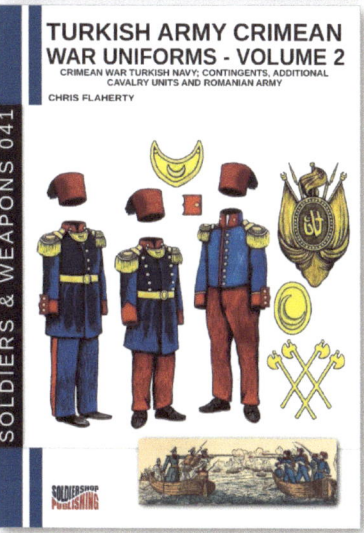

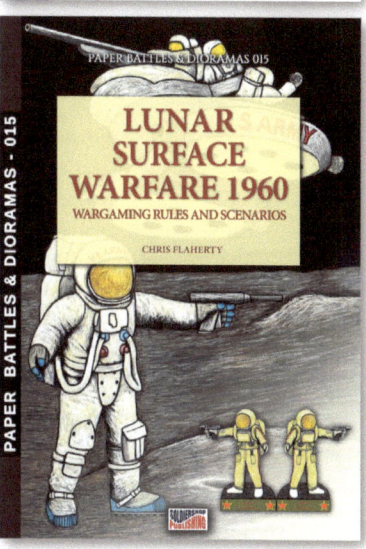

SOLDIERS&WEAPONS 050

www.ingramcontent.com/pod-product-compliance
Lightning Source LLC
LaVergne TN
LVHW071658060526
838201LV00037B/371